MATTHEW BALLEZA
GRINDERS FIND A WAY

Copyright © 2023 by Matthew Balleza

All rights reserved. No part of this publication may be reproduced, stored or transmitted in any form or by any means, electronic, mechanical, photocopying, recording, scanning, or otherwise without written permission from the publisher. It is illegal to copy this book, post it to a website, or distribute it by any other means without permission.

First edition

*This book was professionally typeset on Reedsy.
Find out more at reedsy.com*

For the chiseled twins. You know who you are...

If you can fill the unforgiving minute
With sixty seconds' worth of distance run,
Yours is the Earth and everything that's in it,
And—which is more—you'll be a Man, my son!

- Rudyard Kipling

The news

Let's get the good news out of the way.

The boys were fast. Stupid fast. They were Loyola High's men's cross country team. The stags. Colors red and white. If you had passed these kids in the hall, you might not suspect how fast they were. They resembled most cross country teams. Six fruity white kids with floppy hair, who wore running shoes with khakis to class. They were generally a group of nice guys. They got good grades and good SAT scores. And were all around GOOD.

If you asked their peers to explain what cross country was, how it worked, why some kids chose to run painful laps on repeat, or how the team was doing that year - you would get a lot of blank stares.

It was not football, anyway.

But on paper they were a team poised for glory. That year they were chasing the fourth undefeated season in a row, the first quartet in school history. They were stacked with three of the fastest runners in the state. Paul Stafford, Dave Jones, and Sam Bush - seniors, with scholarships to Oregon, Michigan, and USC. There was no secret to their success. They were well trained, well disciplined. Some said their coach was the best in the nation. Easily the best in the state.

But that's where the good news ends.

One month into the new season, longtime coach and local legend, Bill Press, quit cold turkey, leaving his roster of well groomed runners stranded, shepherdless. There was no grand announcement. No official farewell. Not even a hint. He was there one day, gone the next.

The day it happened, the boys had just finished practice. Tempo runs on the blistering hot track. Afterwards they stretched in a small patch of shade behind the bleachers. All practice Press hadn't shown, and no one had heard from him. That was unusual, but not unheard of. While the others finished stretching, the three captains, Paul, Sam, and Dave ran up to the athletic building to see if they could find him. They assumed he was in his office grading overdue papers, which he sometimes did.

What they found instead was a sheet of school letterhead slapped on the outside of his office door. It said,

Concerning all athletes and staff,

Due to urgent personal matters, Mr. Press has taken leave of his current coaching and teaching responsibilities, effective immediately. We are grateful for his years of service and many accomplishments.

Signed, Mike Nichols, Athletic Director.

For a moment Paul stood there breathless, dumbfounded. He reread it. Then he stripped it off the door, crumpled it, and marched down the hall to the Athletic Director's office. Sam Bush and Dave Jones followed. Paul banged on the door, then banged again, then pushed in without asking.

The AD's name was Mike Nichols. He was a big portly man with a flushed face. He looked up from his computer and raised his hand, as though he were anticipating the intrusion.

Hey guys, I know you're upset.

Upset?! What the hell is going on? Paul demanded. Where's Press? And what's this, he said, uncrumpling the memo.

I'm sorry, Mike said. I can't say much. All I can say is what's written on that memo.

The memo? There's nothing on the memo that says anything. Urgent personal matters. The hell is that?

Nichols shrugged.

Are you trying to tell us Press just up and walked out? Because Bill Press didn't just up and walk out and leave his team with a sheet of paper.

I'm afraid he did just walk out...

That's a bunch of bullshit, Paul said. He stepped forward, the memo in his fist. He hated the bland red face staring back at him. He wanted to swing.

Please calm down, Nichol's said.

Paul...Sam caught his arm. Paul shook it free.

No, get off me Sam. He turned back to Nichols. You can't get rid of a guy who's one of the all time greats at this school. He was coaching when you were in diapers.

I didn't get rid of him.

Then who did?

That's all the questions I can take right now. I'm not at liberty to discuss it...

Discuss what?! What the hell are you talking about? What happened? Where's Press?

Paul. Please. The memo says what I'm able to say.

No! You can't be serious. Press has won more county and state championships than all your football coaches combined. And all you can say is read the memo?? The memo!? You can't be serious.

But he was serious.

Guys, he said, giving a look to Sam and Dave behind Paul.

Come on man, they said to their teammate. They took him by the arm to leave.

As they backed toward the door, Mike said, I'm working right now to bring someone in to sub for him, alright? The reality is, Paul, people come and go. Even the best. Even Press. I'm grateful for all Press did. Really, I am…

While you're here, there's something else I should…he began, but the anger on Paul's face persuaded him against it. Never mind, he said. Any other changes, I'll keep you informed.

Outside the sun was hot and heavy. The air was a furnace. They found the rest of the team waiting by the bleachers, where their patch of shade had dwindled to a wisp. They told them the news. No one said anything. They stood with dumb faces, in the heat that held them in a straightjacket.

So what now? someone said. That's when bewilderment set in. And worry. And of course, rumors.

Gospel of Press

A few thought it was a hoax at first. A test to show them how poorly they ran without a drill sergeant. But they did not need a test to know how quickly they resorted to bitching and bellyaching and bad form. Other rumors surfaced. Some said it was health issues. Kirby joked, Maybe too many pints of potato salad finally caught up to him (shut up, Kirby). Some said he had an affair with another teacher. (who, Ms. Hofsteadder? haha, can you imagine? For a combined age of a hundred and fifty haha). Others said that he was recruited by a division one school. (Nah, he's turned down those offers before. He's too much of a big fish in a small pond.)

On it went for a few days. No news from the AD. What added to the mystery was that some of the runners said they had seen him around town, doing errands. Press was a private man to be sure, but he was not ungentlemanly. He would not give up the whistle without warning. Something else was going on.

A week passed. The three captains took up the slack. Slowly, the initial pangs of abandonment wore off, and the team breathed a sigh of relief. They had their first real break from the furnace of training. It was like coming up out of the water after your head was held under to the point of drowning.

That was not a figure of speech.

The Press season was well known and well hated, but also well respected. He famously called the first month back the *drowning days*. As he put it candidly, if you're not drowning on your own vomit at least twice a week you're not working hard enough.

This was the gospel of Press. And to understand the stags, you had to understand it. His runners knew it and followed it. Even when he was not present they could hear his gravel voice and feel his shadow bulging across the track. They could feel his stare tracing them like a laser pointer. He was a potbellied, mean-eyed General MacArthur. A grade A hardass. He had bushy sideburns that flared under his bucket hat. A face fixed in a squint. An orange whistle that he whipped around his fingers when he talked, and whipped against his thigh when they ran, and whipped at slackers when they slacked.

Before he started coaching he was a cop. His coaching style retained a sense of black and blue street-tough justice. He had three ironclad rules.

1. Don't suck.
2. Don't be a showoff.
3. Don't be a shit.

There was an unspoken fourth rule, but more on that later.

In general, most kids kept the rules. When they didn't, trouble ensued. He liked to say he never wrote the rules down because they were already written on the back of his hand. And he could show you if you forgot. That too was no figure of speech. A few years back it got him in hot water. .

There was a kid on the team named Jack Delaney. He was

fast but he broke rule no. 2. Press overheard him on the bus say, if he wanted to, he could tear the race apart and win the race running backwards smoking a cigarette.

That meet, Middlesburg, he did just that. Jack was so far in the lead, and so cocky, he was half a minute ahead of the nearest runner - he turned around smiling and back pedaled through the finish line, with his fingers to his lips like he was taking a drag. That's when Press tore him apart. Lost his shit, really lost it, Alex said. Called him a conceited ****, a bloodsucking waste of talent, and more expletives. Jack threw a punch that broke Presses jaw - it was a whole thing.

Some parents jumped on him; called him angry, abusive, 'adrenaline addicted'. But many other parents came to his defense. The rest of his team did too. Jack ended up quitting. The whole thing blew over.

It was true that he was all those things they said. But he was also excellent. There was no questioning that. Behind the outburst, there was the pedigree. Dozens of championships, all Americans, ex Olympians - who could all trace a lineage of success back to this man. They called his office 'party city' because of all the awards, banners, accolades, newspaper clippings cluttering the walls.

He was not all bad cop. The runners who came to run got the best training they could ask for. He did not cut people and he did not *weed* them out. He always said that people cut themselves and people weeded themselves out. But he wanted runners. He demanded runners. Runners who ran. Not kids who used running like some 'mambypamby conditioning exercise to tune up for other sports'.

There were other things he had no time for. He had no time for softness. He had seen too much softness in his day. He had seen too many self-claimed *naturals* forfeit their abilities because they never learned how to give it gas. He had seen too many burnouts. *Potential* was another gagword. He wasted no time wondering if one of his runners was going to be a star. He taught a gospel of 'strong will by broken will'. He built up what he broke down, but he always began by breaking down. He drove a wedge between a kid and his comfort. He pummeled pretty runners into Prefontaines.

He chiseled record breakers out of wimps and whiners. He liked to say his runners were not fair-weather striders, but foul weather gluttons. They got fat off other teams' excuses. Rain? Good. Driving rain? Better. Freezing rain? Slashing rain? Carnage on the course? Now we're talking.

His philosophy was his name and his name was his method. He *pressed*. He pressed and he pressed and he punished and he pressed some more. Only then, after a douse of refining fire could he speculate truthfully about any of his runners.

He would bring a bucket to practice and set it at the finish line. When a kid sandbagged it home, he would boot it into the bleachers. If he was really mad, he would grip the runner by the back of their necks and drag them to the starting line, the way you would take an unpottytrained puppy and make it sniff its own you know what….

But when a kid ran well, he did this thing they called the Skippy. It was half a jig where he'd hop in a circle, swinging his orange whistle overhead like a lasso, and howl. That was rare.

Once in a while, after a hard practice, or a big win, he would call a huddle. He would open up his gravel voice and say something like…'Etch it on your brains and in your bones - that feeling of going neck to neck and pulling ahead. That raw feeling of being on the starting line and getting the shakes. That feeling of finding out we're doing speedwork for practice, again. You'll miss it. Ten years from now, when it's Tuesday morning and you're crammed into your cubicle, answering emails and making powerpoint slides for your boss, waiting for five oclock to roll around so you can go home and have a beer on your couch and wake up and do it all over again - You'll miss these days. You'll miss the time you came to the starting and there was nothing between you and victory but lungs and legs and blisters and the earth.

Sandbag the rest of your life for all I care, but not here.

For Press, running was here and now. He believed running was the purest form of athleticism on the face of the Earth. A supreme act of the moment. Medicine to the soul. Steel to the will.

Like all coaches he had his favorites. And if you were good enough, you got a name. *Birddog. Bugbite. Gizzard. Chump...* were a few that came through the years. But one name eclipsed them all. That was Paul Stafford's name. Paul was his prize runner, the embodiment of all he preached. And Press called him *Slobbers*, a name he really loved.

Press and Paul

Some of Presses old runners would come back at the yearend banquet and share how they missed the discipline and the nose to the grindstone. They'd say there are few people in the world who invest in others the way Press invests in his runners. Even if it's painful. Love the hard work now. It will pay off.

Press called this the boomerang effect. Most kids hated him at the start and loved him at the end. But Paul Stafford loved him from the start and loved him all through. Paul was the best runner on the team by bounds and leaps. By the time his senior year came around he was committed to Oregon. He had swept almost every running record in the state, and won nationals twice.

He was one of those stunning athletes who come along once in a decade and whip every ass in town, and remind a coach why they coached. He had that trifecta of talent, discipline, direction. As Press often put it, he was 'a corvette on a country road.' Press enjoyed watching as much as he enjoyed coaching.

Press was like a father to Paul, and Paul was the living testament to his legacy. He was chockfull of Press's mantras, his favorite being, *Grinder's find a way.*

He got his name Slobbers freshman year. Back then, his

mouth hung open when he ran and drooled like a St. Bernard. His face broke into furies down the final stretch. But each year the mouth closed a little more, to the point that calling him Slobbers was comic irony. Even when he was pumping, his mouth was no more than a slit. He had trained his breath to a whistle.

Like Press he had a hot temper, but when Press was around, he was calm and steady. He was captain, moral exemplar. When he talked, guys shut up.

He had two gears. Fast and faster. Physically he was not big, but he was built like an ideal runner: long, strandy, and toned, with veiny legs and tendons that popped off his muscles even when he was standing still. What was big was his confidence. His ego was giant. His teammates called him Big Paul. Calm Paul. Mr. Composure. They called him The Machine. Big Staff. Big Stick. Big You know what. And he seemed to have all that. At least when Press was around.

More impressively, he bridged a gap which was highly unbridgeable for most high school cross country kids. He was one of the popular kids in school. He had grafted onto the football team, the soccer team, the lacrosse team. He was up for two or three senior superlatives, including Best All Around..

You would think Best All Around would have an inside lane to Press. That he could call up his mentor and master and find out what was going on. But it didn't work. He called and he called and never got through. He knew where Press lived. He drove by the house and knocked, but no one came to the door. By all appearances the house was empty.

Without any good answers, without any word further from Mike Nichols, Calm Paul began to unravel. Every time the team walked past the athletic offices, Paul would raise his voice and say something like, Nichols is pure bogus. He's an embarrassment. He's fake news. How the hell does that guy ever get to be athletic director? Sitting there in his big Costco pants and bag of Ruffles…he's covering something up just to protect his own fat ass.

With Press gone, the question was not, what would happen to the team, but what would happen to Paul.

And sure enough they began to see.

Team retreat

Every year around that time the team took a trip up to Maine and rented a small cabin near an empty stretch of stony beach called Flamingo Beach. They took the trip to reset, to rest, to regroup, to put their legs on ice and escape the fiery furnace of Bill Press.

It was a tradition, and that year they needed it more than ever.

They were in the woods. A quarter mile inland from the lonely shore. The phone service was spotty and the closer they got the road signs turned to strips of hand painted wood board hammered on trees. In terms of neighbors, there were a few tiny hippie looking bungalows close by, but not much. There was also a rough strip of trailer homes with Warning, Dog, signs, but they never went there. A mile down the beach there was a humongous mansion called Foxhall. Every morning for their run the team trespassed on its lush hills. It was a large empty looking castle, with heaps of overgrown gables and big hedges of herbs and wildflowers.

Trespassing Foxhall, wondering who lived there, and who on the team was going to marry the rich daughter of the family they imagined owned it (Paul, of course), was the extent of their luxury accommodations. Their cabin was rustic and log built. It lacked hot water. It lacked central air. It lacked warmth in general. There were no bedrooms, just a main room with two big picnic tables, two small windows, and a narrow set of stairs that climbed to the loft attic where they slept on the ground in sleeping bags. The bare kitchen was a propane stove and a fridge and a sink with tap water that smelled like eggs. No microwave, no toaster, no oven. A lacquer of old yellow grease covered the wall behind the stove and a dry moth-eaten curtain hung above the window above the sink.

From the kitchen you could see the sawdust outhouse through the steep slope of woods. No one used the outhouse, which sank into its own pile of sawdust and looked like a haunted porta-potty. For number two, the deal was: go anywhere. Bring paper towels. For number one, there was a designated spot. A robust mulberry bush that Sam Bush christened his freshman year, and called henceforth The Pee Bush. It was their urinal. It was their pee bush.

This is where they went. To the sticks of Maine, to the sticks of a cabin. Every year they griped when they arrived, and doubted whether they should go somewhere new the next year. Every year it rained. Every year someone suggested better accommodations, more sunshine, more vitamin D…and every year they got this place. Every year they packed too little food and too much booze. Every year they were three blankets short. Every year someone (Tits) forgot undies. Every year someone puked or someone blacked out. One year someone (Dave) stripped down to their skivvies and climbed a tree and ran the next meet with poison ivy burning their crotch. Every year stupid bets were made and stupid games were played. Every year stupid things were said and stupid things were done. And every year they got this place.

It was cheap and it was rough. Its cheapness and roughness appealed to the boys. They grew whiskers on their chin. Their legs got bushy. They ditched deodorant for a few days, and came out the other end feeling like men of the woods. It all washed out in the end. They soon got used to it. For all it lacked, it had one thing going for it. It was good luck. Whenever they came back, they went on a tear. They cleaned house…

It was pitch black and raining hard when they arrived. They came up to the porch and a weak floodlight flickered on and they could see the water dancing down the log chinks and pooling in the gravel lot.

As Paul came in he smacked the top of the door frame and found the light switch. He yelled out, There's only one rule under this roof. Poor man's Vegas, baby. What happens on retreat stays on retreat.

Run

Early the next morning the boys ran to Foxhall. The air was cold and the sky was pale blue. It rained still, and there were crooked gashes and wet gullies over the earth. They ran through the woods, through thistle and scrub, toward the old belfry on the windy lookout point on the east lawn of the mansion. The closer they got they could smell the sea below. They ran uphill, into the spitting rain. Their shorts were damp at the thighs and their swift clean strides made a tsk-tsk-tsk in the long grass. Seven of them came in single file, with Paul leading the charge and two stragglers battling it out for last place.

It was a race to the top. Last one in got hazed…

Paul was first up. He rang the bell. Then he made a flat whistle with his teeth. The pace picked up. One after another came in. Sam, Dave, Tyson, Tits, each ringing the bell in his turn. The single file line split into a boisterous crowd of whoops and ass slaps. Paul whistled again. His co-captains, Sam Bush and Dave Jones, stood beside him hollering down at Kirby, aka the ginger haired giant, who battled Jimmy Morales, aka Momo.

Beat his ass, Momo, beat his ass! Sam yelled. Dave yelled, Grinders find a way! Grinders find a way! Pick it up boys.

Last one in gets buried in the rocks.

As Kirby and Momo closed the gap, their foot race became a tangle of arm swings and thrown elbows. They fought against the slope and against the wet grass and against one another. Momo inched ahead, then Kirby tugged the tail of his shirt and they were neck to neck, elbow to elbow.

Momo, who spoke Spanish but rarely used it around gringos, started shouting out FUERTE! FUERTE! FUERTE! like some kind of mind trick. The team egged him on. Give it to him Momo, give it to him! Ay Ay! In the last hundred meters he stuck his foot out and made a nasty swipe sideways and the giant tripped, sprawled out flat on the grass and ate a face full of scrub.

Momo dug up the final stretch and rang the bell.

Last one in, Paul said to Kirby. You do the honors.

Kirby pushed up from the ground. He cleared a snot rocket and placed his hands on his hips. He was still panting, still pissed at the dirty swipe. His big skinny legs were red with grassburn. Coming forward he glanced at Momo, who was bent over, weary with laughter. You dirty bastard, he said. Fuerte, my ass…

They all declared it was a clean swipe, even if it was a dirty swipe. Now ring that bell, they shouted, Ring that bell.

Kirby made his walk of shame and rang the bell. Before he had time to catch his breath, someone pantsed him to his ankles and they all scattered, skipping down the bluff, yeehawing and screaming penis and look at that skinny little white kid and his skinny little ding dong, and every other thing you would expect to hear on a men's high school cross country team.

Rumors

When they got back, Dave saw he had three missed calls from Mike Nichols and a handful of overdue messages that had just arrived from poor cell service. While the team was cooling down, he stepped onto the driveway and called him back.

I've been trying to call you since last night, Mike said.

Sorry about that, the reception is spotty out here.

Anyway, I got two pieces of news for you, for the team. First is, I found a step-in coach for you guys. His name is Cal Brennan. He's young and he's got a different style than Press...you'll see. I've met him already and he's a good guy. I think you'll like him. He'll be starting this coming Wednesday. The other thing I wanted to share is that you guys are going to have a new teammate. West coast transfer.

We already got a full roster, Dave said, and there's no JV.

Sam stepped out onto the porch and saw Dave drifting carefully away from the cabin. He overheard bits of the phone call. He stepped down and started after him, curious to hear what was going on.

Yes, I know, Mike said. It's not perfect and I'm not completely certain how it's going to work. There was a whole mix up with the timing. The west cross country's season is different than ours, and when he was transferring, all the stuff with Bill was…

The call began to break up. Dave moved around trying to get a better signal, but all he got were bits and pieces…

…. says he's pretty fast…name is F…Sun

…told him where you're staying… and he should get there…

Dave…there? you get that…?

…tell you first so… decide…share it with the others…Paul in particular.

The call went flat. Fortunately, he could piece enough together to share with Sam, who was there beside him, invested in the call. They made their way up to the cabin, talking low.

Well? Sam said.

Dave flipped his phone in the air. He said, Apparently we got fresh blood coming in. New coach and new guy on the team.

Wait, what?! How's…

I don't know, that's all I know. Coaches name is Cal something, and new guy is a transfer from the west coast. Didn't get his name. Begins with an F. He was breaking up. But he might be coming?

Coming where?

Coming here.

Like up here, to the cabin?

Sounded like it. But I don't know.

Why'd he call you and not…you know who, first? Sam said, turning his head to the cabin.

Probably because he wants us to diffuse it a little. Let it sink in some…

Sink in some? Good luck with that. It's gonna go off like…

Tits came outside to pee at the bush. He looked at them, saw the serious looks on their faces. Dave and Sam went quiet.

Good luck, huh? Tits said. I know what you guys are talking about.

You do not, Dave said. Finish up peeing and get out of here.

Tits giggled. I do. I bet I do.

What do you think you know?

I don't *think,* I know, I *know* I know…He's coming, isn't he?

He was talking with his back to them and his belly to the bush.

Tits, Sam said, raising his foot. I'm about to push you into this bush…

Hey, all I'm saying is I heard about it, that's all…

The front door clapped and Paul strut out. Heard about what? he said.

Nothing, Sam said. Tits is just out here being a turd. Making up shit.

I'm not making up shit…

About what? Paul said, looking at the other two.

Tits shook himself and raised his eyebrows at Dave and Sam, and quickly hopped back up the stairs. You can ask them about what. I'm not the one keeping secrets…

They took a deep sigh. Then they said, Come with us.

Begins with an F

There were two ways it could have gone. The first way was an explosion followed by a hush. The second was a hush followed by an explosion. They got the second.

The moment they began to tell him, they could see the storm brewing in his eyes, the news eating its way into him. He was livid, but he tried to keep himself calm by listening and nodding slowly and looking at the ground. He folded his arms and body looked tense as a kinked hose.

When he swallowed the whole pill, he took a sharp inhale and looked up.

How does Tits know? he said.

He doesn't, Sam said. He just came outside and overheard us.

I was just about to tell you, Dave said. I had just gotten off the phone with Mike. He figured he'd call me first, because if he talked to you, you'd tear him to shreds.

Paul spat. That's probably the one smart thing he's done since I've known him, he said. And you don't know the new guy's name?

Nope. Begins with an F. The call was scratchy.

What's his deal? He's not coming here, is he? Paul asked.

Sam looked at Dave. Dave gave a timid shrug and made his white lie.

I doubt it, Dave said. There'd be no way of him even finding this place, either.

Let's leave it at that then, Paul said. It's enough upheaval for one season. And let's not let the cat out while we're here. I don't want any more of them asking questions, running their traps. Agreed?

Agreed.

Talk

After lunch the rain cleared. Some of them went outside and others stayed in. But it did not take long for the news to float. Paul walked down to the water by himself to clear his head. When he came back, he caught part of Tits and Momo shooting the breeze.

…All I'm saying, Tits said, is that he rolled up to the AD office in a brand new benz.

Why does that make him a chump? Momo replied.

I'm not saying he's a chump…

Just because Press rode around in a beater, doesn't mean-

They looked up. They could feel Paul's presence looming.

Shut up both of you, Paul said. Don't talk about stuff you have no knowledge of or business in.

I think we all have business in it, Paul, Tits said. We are a team after all. And we are getting a new coach…

Is that what you guys were out there talking about? Kirby joined in. I saw him come in last week to meet with Mike Nichols.

Paul opened his mouth. He was about to yell, but he caught himself and shut his mouth and counted off five seconds before speaking again.

Tits, we're done speculating.

We're not speculating.

Tits, Paul raised his voice…DONE.

Hey, don't you want to know Paul? It's your senior season, anyway.

Tits had a way of driving Paul insane with his innocent comments and mild prods. That last comment hit a nerve, and Paul made his sharp inhale, like he was trying with all his might to contain his anger.

Not right now, I don't. Right now I want to be fast, and I want our team to be fast. So shut up for right now.

An hour passed and soon enough he heard the two of them at it again. He was about to walk out the door and let it go when he heard Tits drop his voice, I bet you he's coming tonight.

The very mention stopped Paul in his place. His hands clenched at his side. He could feel his anger swelling in his gut, but he tried something new this time. He laughed.

Tits, are you serious? You're still talking about stuff you don't know. What are you talking about, someone coming? Did you invite someone? If you did, I hope it's someone of the opposite sex. Otherwise, cut it out

I'm not making anything up. I'm telling you what I heard.

Oh yeah, from who?

My brother, who's on the baseball team. He said yesterday some kid he didn't know asked him if he knew any of the guys on the cross country team. My brother asked who he was, and the guy said he was a transfer who was going to be joining our team. My brother told him we were up here, on team retreat.

Paul smiled. Are you done making shit up?

I'm not full of shit. I'm telling you he's coming.

Right…sure he is Tits. Because apparently you know more than the captains about what's going on with the team…

He's coming Paul.

Who, your male stripper, right?

Stop being a dick. Just cause you're a captain doesn't mean…

Tits…SHUT. UP. Before I kick you in the balls.

And that he was the fastest kid in the country if he wanted to be.

Too bad he doesn't. And too bad he's too busy being poor and living in shit subsidized housing and having no Daddy and getting every ugly girl he lays eyes on pregnant.

Paul, Sam cut in. From outside he could overhear the conversation taking a bad turn. Let him be, he's just talking. Tits, Sam said, take a break and stop talking about whatever you're talking about.

No, I'm tired of getting pushed around for nothing. Why don't you tell him then, Sam?

Tell who what?

Tell Paul, that the new guy is coming here, too-night.

Paul laughed out loud, looked at Sam for reassurance of bullshit. Sam laughed too. He said, I think we're all getting a little stir crazy. Let's get outside.

Tits said, Laugh all you want. He'll be here.

Paul killed his laughter. He shoved Tits into Momo, then he said, Get out of here fatty. Go talk to a tree.

Dogbite

Not twenty minutes passed when Paul called the team together and ordered a surprise run.

When? Tyson asked.

Now, Paul said.

My legs are shot from earlier, Momo said. We already did our hard run.

I wouldn't call what you did earlier, hard, Momo. Gear up boys…

When they were dressed and ready to go, he dragged the team onto the road and they ran. The air was thick with fog. It was a sloppy run to start. The team was still recovering from their earlier run and lunch had not settled. Sure enough, not long after they started Paul began to push the pace. Without warning he went faster and faster until the pace broke the team into twos and threes.

Even Sam and Dave struggled to keep up. They were close enough to hear Paul muttering things to himself. He did not look back once, except to shout in a vengeful voice, Pick it up, Pick it up!

Through the woods he blazed a convoluted route they had never run before. It was like he had no set run in mind, no clear destination. He was running them to run them ragged.

The farther they went down unknown trails, and the harder Paul pushed, the more his cocaptains fell back some and began to fear the change coming over their friend.

Paul, you wanna ease up some? I think we lost some of the guys back there...Sam called out.

Good! Tell em to catch up...

His stride became heavier, his breathing louder. They could feel him tightening his grip, inflicting them with the pace and misdirection. They came to a fork in the path. The left led back to their cabin, the right crossed into the creepy looking shanty of trailer homes. Down that alley, BEWARE: DOG signs hung askew from every fence.

They had never gone right before. But this time they went right. From the rear, Momo and Tits could see the foggy outline of Tyson and Kirby ahead of them bending toward the dismal looking alley. The clusters of runners stretched apart further. Tits called out for them to slow up, but all he could hear in reply was a series of muffled shouts.

Paul and the captains made it through. Tyson and Kirby made it through. At the end of the dirt alley the path took a hard right, but the air was so thick with fog, Momo and Tits missed it and veered into an awkward clearing of woodchip and crabgrass. They stopped and looked around, but it was too late before they realized they had strayed into a yard, or something like a yard. A chain somewhere shook. As they retreated, they saw the outline of a white dog with brown splotches, moving. It was chained by a green clothesline. The sound of their intrusion had roused it from its post. With a growl that turned quickly to loud snapping barks, it barreled toward them. The dog was no fido. It was a pitbull with black eyes and a menacing pink muzzle. They ran as fast as they could, but Momo tripped at the edge of the clearing and the dog caught up and snapped before Tits had time to help. The dog bit him on the leg, and would have kept biting, had it not been for Tits' thrown shoes, one after another. Then a hooded figure appeared behind the fog and the green clothesline jerked and the dog disappeared, leaving the two runners alone on the dirt track.

Tits shouted out to Kirby and Tyson or anyone to stop and come back. He collected his thrown shoes and as he put them on together they examined the damage. Momo cursed under his breath, his eyes switching from his wound to the edge of the road, to see if anyone came. His leg bled freely from the outside of his knee down his calf and into his shoe. Bite marks dented the area. The skin was peeled in flaps and a chunk of meat was missing.

It was a long game of telephone getting the message up to Paul, but eventually it got there. Sam caught up with him and told him what happened.

Tell him to meet us on the hills and keep going, Paul said.

The rest of the team's back there. Kirby and Tyson turned back. Should we…?

No, that's good enough. We don't need everyone there to baby him. He should've kept up and watched those stupid signs anyway. Unless he's on the ground bleeding out, which I doubt he is…

Momo lay in the dust a half mile back. His flank, shirt, shorts and socks were a bloody mess. Tyson removed his shirt and wrapped it around his knee and tied it in a knot.

Do we need to take you somewhere? Kirby said, squatting.

Closest civilized place is an hour out, Tits said. Our best shot right now is if you can stand Momo, let's get it cleaned first. And I got pain killers and I saw a first aid kit at the cabin.

Momo tried extending his leg and grimaced. I think I'm fine, if you can just help me up and get me back.

Tyson took him on one side and Kirby on the other. They lifted him gingerly to his feet. Tits followed behind, carrying Momo's removed shoe. They walked back toward the fork in the road. They took the left and headed to the cabin. The whole way back, Momo swore in Spanish. The others kept quiet. At one point Tyson heard the phrase, '…fucking dog, and he said to Momo, I'd be just as pissed as you if that dog came after me….

Momo looked at him, shook his head. He said, It's not the dog I'm talking about…

Up to speed

They knew who he was talking about. And they all felt it. When they got back, the captains were still out.

He's losing his shit, Tits said. Can't even stop to check on his own man. Calls another run, even though we're supposed to be resting. Rabbits out in front of everybody. Ever since we got here, he's been hot and cold. I feel like he's about to do something he regrets. He goes from being completely silent and composed to taking over every conversation and telling everybody what they should be talking about and what they shouldn't be talking about. He's picking fights, looking for someone to smack upside the head. Then he tries to hoo-rah everybody together. I'm tired of it.

Kirby said, He was fine until he got the news of the coach and the new guy. That set him off. You had to stir him up, Tits, didn't you, telling him the new guy's coming…?

Tits shook his head. He's about to be stirred up either way. He can think whatever he wants, but he'll get quiet the moment he realizes I'm not making anything up. Sorry to disrupt his perfect little season.

Meanwhile the captains had been running the hills. Sam and Dave left early to check on Momo, leaving Paul to stay and finish them by himself. When they arrived, the rest of the team quit talking. Momo sat on the ground wiping his leg, wincing as he flexed it. Tyson cleaned his wound with hose water. They dried it first with a bath towel, then staunched it further with paper towels and gauze from the first aid kit. They smeared neosporin on it, then folded more gauze over it and taped the whole wad down with white athletic tape.

Momo held a grocery bag filled with loose ice and ice water taken from the beer cooler to his wound. He elevated his leg on a duffle bag. He shut his eyes and washed down three expired tylenol from the first aid kit with a bottle of powerade. Tits stayed with him acting as his helper, and the group effectively disbanded because of the situation.

When Paul came back, he went straight into the cabin without saying a word. A few minutes later he came out, not smiling and not frowning. He stared at Momo and Tits and the rest of them lazing around. They could not read his expression. Paul had a small square face, a face remarkable not only because of how tightly his eyes and his nose and his mouth packed together, but by how lined it was for so young a man. Droplets of sweat stood on the ridge of his eyebrows.

He came over to Momo, wiped his hand across his face. How's your little boo boo? he said. As he said this he whipped his shirt off and struck it softly at him as if he were joking.

Momo said nothing. He shifted the bag of ice on his leg and Tits helped him straighten his leg. Paul watched them closely and intensely.

You two make quite the pair. Quite the act. What's Tits, your nurse? Huh,Tits? You sitting here telling him sweet things to make his boo boo feel better? You changing his wraps out for him like a good old nurse?

What's your problem? Tits said, facing Paul. Why are you

joking right now? He's your teammate and he got mauled by a dog, because of your stupid run.

Because of me? I doubt that. Unless I told you to go chasing after a pitbull. If you would have kept up with the rest of us you'd have seen the trail and we wouldn't have any issues. He pointed his finger at Momo's leg.

And I wouldn't call that mauled. That's a scrape, buddy. While you were cleaning off a scrape, which you earned by being slow, we were up there working our tails off. Me, Sam, and Dave. The only three guys on this team going places with our running. You could have kept us together if you would have picked up your slack. But I look around and the two of you are slacking like always.

Momo was huffing, chewing his lips in anger. Do you hear yourself? Right now? You're the one that started running down that straightway, not to mention took us down that chicken shit alley when that stupid dog came and got me. Why'd you do that? We never ran there before.

Paul wiped his forehead with his shirt. Don't moan, he said. Get your sloppy mess cleaned up. And tell me you're not using ice from our coolers?

Give him a break, Paul, Kirby spoke up.

Shut up, Kirb, get out of here. You two clean your slop up, stop using our ice, and get up to speed for once.

Captain's meeting

Shortly, Sam called a captain's meeting on the front drive. Being the peacekeeper of the team, he spoke first. He said, Paul, I'd go easy on Tits and Momo if I were you.

Easy? Easy for what?

They're upset about the dogbite and all the…he hesitated.

The what? Paul said.

All the new stuff going on. New coach, new addition to the team…

Oh come on, you make it sound like I've been making heads rolls. Sorry I'm not here to pamper these kids. Last thing we need is Tits going around making shit up.

What if he's not making it up though, Dave said.

Paul turned Dave and said, Come on Dave, not you too.

Paul had a wet hand towel draped over his neck. He took it off and passed it through a hole he made with his thumb and pointer, over and over.

See, this is what happens, he said, shaking his head, Everybody loses their head when change comes. Everybody starts gaggling like geese and getting bogus injuries and forgetting what comes first. Which is running. Enough speculating who's running and who's not, and who's coming and who's not, and who's coaching and who's not. Enough with the rumor mill.

His voice grew louder. Then it dropped and he changed his expression. A dirty grin snuck into his cheek. He made the towel dance on the palm of his hand. He lifted his eyes. For all I know, he said, the change could be good. Sam's mom could step in as coach and I'd be just fine with that.

Paul, come on, man, Sam said. The guys inside aren't happy…

No, forget about them a sec, he said. They can whine all they want for all I care. We *are* on retreat. We gotta loosen up some, maybe that's the issue. The grin slid from left cheek to right. He looked at Dave, to try and draft him into his dirty thought. I can see it on Dave's face too, he said. He's thinking the same thing I am. I wouldn't mind if Miss Bush got us doing some fartleks. Couple tempos, couple *hills*…

Sam shook his head. He said to Paul, You're saying two different things. Sending two different vibes. You're saying we gotta be no nonsense, 'we're here to run' on one hand, and on the other we gotta loosen up, not take things so seriously, 'we're on retreat'.

What's your point? Paul said.

Just…I don't know. I'm just checking in, I guess. Making sure you're ok, you're alright with everything.

Paul made a hard snuff through his nose. The dirty grin fell away and he quit dancing the towel on his hand. He threw it round his neck again and resumed his angry tone.

Well I appreciate you coming out here to check on me and my *feels*. If that's what your intent was. You too, Dave. But I'm not sending two messages. I'm sending one message and it's the same one Press would be sending if he was around, which is: work hard, play hard. Simple. You know that. But right now our group of softies isn't doing either. They work soft and they play soft. And then when I get on them for not doing it, the whining starts.

The towel came off again and he began wrapping it round his fist as he talked.

I promise you one thing, this team is not going to get anywhere this season if we expect some no name coach and some no name sandbagger to come and sabotage what Press built. Hell no. No one's going to rescue us from the season. I'll tell you one thing if we're going to run like hell the rest of the season and get our victory lap in, it'll be on our watch, not on rumors and grapevines. Got it? Got it…

He made another hard snuff. He paced a little way away from them, and turning his back, lapsed into a bitter silence. He flapped the towel into his palm. Then he walked toward the cabin and sat down on the lowest step of the stairs. He stared off into the foggy woods. The wind blew soft tufts of pine needles to the edge of the road. He brooded for a long time, kicking the gravel under his feet away until he sat over a patch of powdery dust.

The others went in and he waited there a long time, until it began to get dark. Then he got up and started making some noise.

Guards down

Outside the fog thickened and thinned and thickened some more. It was symbolic of the heavy mood that swirled through the cabin. In separate rooms the guys played cards, napped, listened to music, and continued their private conversations.

Around nine oclock, Paul ordered everyone to the main living room to do shots. The guys left their hideouts and regrouped along the wall. In the middle of the room, Paul had cleared the picnic table and pushed the benches against the wall. He set two amber handles of bottom shelf bourbon and cinnamon whiskey on the table and poured a flight into a set of neon shot glasses.

All right, he said. He cleared his nostril on the open floor. Before we do our primal scream tonight, we've got some matters to attend to.

First up, it's time to wet the whistle a bit and take some edge off. Some need that edge off more than others.

Momo sat on the floor with his leg extended and a bag of melted ice wrapped around. Paul walked up to him and smirked. He flared his hip and flapped his tongue in a seductive way.

Some of you have been bitching like girls and it's time to

get back to what we came out here to do.

Paul went and grabbed the bottle of Advil sitting on the kitchen counter.and chucked it at Momo.

Take a couple more of those, he said. We need you in the action, Momo.

What are we doing? Tits asked.

Good question Tits, Paul said. His red eyes glazed over them and he licked his lips wet.

We're letting our guards down, leaving our egos at the doormat and having a good time. Having a real good time. We've had a shit year so far. Rumors are flying and coach is missing. So we're going to drink, and play poker, and primal scream, and bury the giant, and whatever the hell we want, and see if your little guy doesn't show up like you've been saying, Tits…Does that sound good? Good.

Unhinged

Within an hour their shirts were off and half of them had tied them around their heads like turbans. The other half were wearing them over their shoulders. They sat at the table playing poker, sipping warm bottom shelf, scratching their bony chests, eating moon pies and chewing bags of salty sunflower kernels.

They all tried to rebound, for Paul's sake more than anyone's.

Big brown beetles chopped against the overhead light and mid game one of them sailed into a shot glass. Paul stopped the game. Smiling, he stood and lifted the neon glass to the light. He said, Who's the man who's gonna throw this back and grow some fuzz? He looked around, offered the glass. No takers? he said, No takers? He shrugged, then threw it back himself, and sat back down and smacked the table and said, Deal me up.

They played one game and took a break. Momo sat on the ground and Tits refilled his ice bag with the remains from their beer cooler. As the night wore on, the wound got worse, and Paul got worse. When Momo peeled away the soaked gauze to check the wound, the swollen flesh was a nasty shade of purple with yellow pus. Soon he began to shiver with a fever. He chewed four more pain killers in quick succession and washed them down with fireball and the eggsmelling tap water. For food they were cleaned out but for a box of booze scented Cheez-its, nutty bars, more sunflower seeds, and a half dozen individual butter packets left in the fridge from who knows when. Momo ate the butter for sustenance, and the rest divided the rest.

At the start of the second game, the team was tipsy. Paul threw back another shot of cinnamon whiskey and yelled out to Momo and Tits, who were still talking on the floor, Why don't you two girls pick your panties up and get up here and stop having your little heart to heart. Get up here, Momo, Don't tell me you're still hobbling around with that fake.

Despite their tipsiness, the team had enough sense to realize the real game that night was not poker. The real game was called Contain Paul Stafford, or Survive Paul Stafford. And they were losing.

They began a second game, but it went off track quickly. Scrounging for food, Kirby had found a single wax candle in the bottom drawer of the kitchen and he lit on the picnic table because he said (and the team agreed) it smelled like PITS everywhere.

They had not played two hands when Paul, with a drunken chuckle, took his card and lit it on the candle and let it burn to a brown stub in his finger. He waved the smoky stub around and said, There, that gets rid of the PITS. Then he rubbed the soot out and smeared the table black and painted two football streaks under his eyes.

He put his other card down, slapped it against the table, and cleared his voice dramatically. He grabbed the cards from all of his teammates and jumbled them in a mish mash on the table. Grabbing the shoulders of Tyson and Sam, who sat next to him, he mounted the bench, then mounted the table top, rising until his head was level with the overhead light. He took the fixture and pointed it outward, using it first like a floodlight to shine on the faces of his teammates, and then like a microphone from which to deliver some speech. His face was red and swollen. His eyes bulged in their sockets.

I think we all know we got someone to celebrate, who we wish was here with us. We all owe a debt to. That's to our old compadre, Bill Press, who taught us well and trained us well. Trained us to win through fair weather and foul weather and never pussy out. Bill Press who said Grinders find a way. And they do. Bill Press, who that dickhead, Mike Nichols -

Paul! Sam shouted, to redirect.

Right…right…Paul slurred. Bill Press who…who, never once let me have a crack at Sadie…

Paul! Sam shouted again, to redirect. Come on…

No, no, let me finish, he said, pulling the light up to his chin. Sadie Press… his hot, hot, daughter, who he told me in private once if anyone was worthy of her it was me. But he still never let me…

Paul! Finish up!

Alright. Bill Press…who, who… left without a word or a warning and just, just…

In an upwelling of drunken emotion his eyes watered and his teeth clenched in his jaw. He became lost in emotion.

Paul! Sam said, tapping him on the leg. Let's finish up.

Paul snapped out of it. He was getting tearful. He looked aside at Sam and said, Sorry, you're right…

Then turning on his jokes again, he said, I do wanna give one more nod to Mrs. Bush, who of all the moms of all the guys on this team is by far the…

It was going down that road again. Before he could say anything more, Dave grabbed his ankle to pull him down but Paul reared back, said Get off me, and drove his heel down, smashing Dave's two fingers.

While Dave shook the pain out, Paul looked around, laughing. In his power-drunk, drunk-drunk state, he could not read the room. No one met him in the eye. Everyone looked down or looked off to the side, and everyone secretly hoped he would stop; stop pushing the envelope; stop pressing his will into every conversation and every situation. The mood of the trip was felt clearly in that moment, which made it different from years past. Every year there was debauchery, but the debauchery was lighthearted. Every year there was hazing, but the hazing was harmless.

Something possessed Paul. Something that could only be called a desire to go out with a bang. What was happening? Here was the moral exemplar descending to a moral pit. Here was Joe cool. Joe smooth. The son of the town judge, known for his level eyes, straight back, and controlled intensity. Here was the steady work horse. The kid who kept his mouth shut when everybody else was complaining. The obedient, diligent, rule following, no bullshit captain. The honor student. Best all around. Pride of the program. State champ. Now unraveling, unhinged, eyes bulging like the pitbull.

There was something else unusual about Paul which they all noticed when they were at pains not to make eye contact with him. He had a small cavity under his sternum. A small pocket of skin that went out and in with his breath like a frog's throat. When it went in, the skin darkened and he looked like he had a hole in his chest. The more he talked, the more he slurred, the more words came out, and profanity spilled like liquor.

So also the truth came.

The room went quiet.

Paul left the light swinging overhead. He squatted on the table and poured a sloppy flight of shots which ran over the edge onto the floor. Across the sticky puddle he said hoarsely, All right, all right, I'm finished for now. But here's to blood, sweat, and, and…He couldn't find the last word, so he added instead, Here's to running like stags.

When he got down they took another break. They finished the food and peed in the pee bush. By the time midnight rolled around, a third sloppy game was about to begin. The team looked like a box of rotten pears. They were beaten, bruised, covered in dried sweat and glazed over. Dave Jones and Sam Bush were no good contradicting the whirling jackhammer that was shirtless Paul Stafford drunk off his ass. They did not know how much more of it they could take.

But they did not need to worry about it.

Tits held his phone up and said, He's almost here. I told you.

Paul said, Who's that?

Tits pointed to the door. Shortly, a beam of headlights swept through the front window. The crunch of gravel. A car door opened and closed. Footsteps, then a knock at the door.

Felix, Nalgene, Primal Scream

He was there waiting for them on the porch steps, his duffle bag in his hand and his figure backlit by the porch light. He cast a lean shadow down the staircase. When the door opened, shirtless Paul stood blocking the entrance, wiping his whiskey hands on his shorts. The team gathered behind him, each looking on to see who it was.

Who are you, Paul said.

I'm Felix. Felix Sun. I'm new to the team. Sorry I'm late. I just got in this week. I heard the team was staying here. There were no signs coming in, so I followed the light and the noise.

He stepped forward and put his hand out to shake, but Paul dodged it by looking inside at the team.

Well good for you. Glad you made it. Feel free to hang out here and get your bag unpacked. We're going to head for a bit and do some team stuff here right now but will be done in a little bit. Boys, he called behind him, Welcome…He turned back, said, What's your name again?

Felix.

Felix, you heard that boys?

Paul stepped aside and the new guy came into the pit smelling cabin, stepping over wet sneakers, bloody shirts, and disposable shot glasses. Momo, with his wet bag of ice, nodded at him from the floor.

He got a couple more nods, a couple heys, but for a minute or so no one said much of anything. He stood in the middle of the big room, him looking at them and them looking at him.

He did not match their lean build. He was lanky, slight, soft. Not to Paul's eyes a runner. At least, not a Press-style runner, with muscle and burst. His ethnicity was unclear. Asian? Polynesian? Some half breed? He was tan skinned, with a baby face and narrow, sleepy looking eyes. He had a mild expression and talked mildly and used mild gestures. Paul hated mild. He equated mild with weak.

He wore a breezy Hawaiian shirt and capri length trousers and checkered slip on Vans. A bright fringe of orange hair stuck out from under a flat billed skater hat. His outfit looked like a cross between a California hippie and a Japanese teen punk.

The staring moments were not the warmest welcome a guy could receive. The team was a bit stunned by his presence, and somewhat shamed by the state of the cabin. On top of that they were tipsy, shirtless, starved.

At last, Sam spoke up. This is it. Welcome. It's a mess right now, hope you don't mind. Throw your bag anywhere you like upstairs. Unfortunately the only bathroom is outside, and we're kind of low on tp, but we're only here till tomorrow so hopefully we can hold out. And, as far as food goes we're cleaned out.

Sorry about that.

That's alright, Felix said, I brought some snacks and stuff. I ate on the way up. I still got half a pie in the car if you guys are interested.

As he looked around, the eyes in the room got big and they

all lurched forward like a herd of hungry cattle.

All but Paul.

Paul, for whatever reason - because Felix was new, or because he was *there*, or because his name was Felix, or because of his capri length pants - did not like him from the moment he saw him. And he abstained from food, though he was starving too, as an act of defiance.

Felix left and came back with a giant box of new york slice pepperoni. The team devoured it. The food broke the ice. The friendliness picked up. The energy picked up. They learned he was a senior from Ventura California. His family had moved for a new job. But before they could learn more, Paul put an end to it.

He said, All right girls, who's ready for some fun? Are we finally ready for the proceedings to begin? You ready Kirby?

Kirby was eating a slice of pizza. Mid bite he looked up, confused.

What proceedings? he asked with his mouth full.

I'm glad you asked. Hopefully you didn't forget you gotta pay for coming in last up the hill. There's a big pile of rocks out there with your name on it.

As he was chewing his slice and chewing the idea, Paul went up to him and restrained his hands behind his back. His pizza fell from his mouth. Dave and Sam came over and helped hold him while the big kid fought and struggled. Paul wrapped his wrists with a roll of duct tape. More guys came and restrained him. The laughter grew. Even Kirby laughed. They brought a handle of whiskey, shot glasses, a blue nalgene bottle. They bound his legs. With three on each side they hoisted the giant ginger out of the cabin and down onto the skinny path that led to the ocean.

Felix followed behind.

Paul said to Felix, Feel free to hang out here while we're doing this...

May I come? he asked.

Paul hesitated. Sam whispered something across Kirby, and Paul said, Alright, but just don't get in the way.

To Paul, Felix was an afterthought, and he made that clear by launching into his hazing scheme with gusto.

The night was cool and the fog cleared. Moonlight bent through the tops of the trees. Through the dark wall of tree trunks they could hear the surf thumping. Two phone flashlights bobbed along, marking the way. They went slowly. Slow enough that Momo, who was dialed up with Advil, could limp alongside and feed the giant from the end of his unfinished pepperoni slice.

On the fumes of their spent legs they dragged him whelping and chewing over soft pine needles to a clearing at the entrance of the beach and set him down at the foot of a pile of white pavement rocks.

Kirby had no fight left. He sat down resigned, chewing his soggy slice like a cud.

The team circled him. Felix and Momo stood just outside the circle, looking in. Catching his breath, Paul picked up a handful of stones and pitched them into the woods. Then he poured dribbles of Evan Williams into a shot glass and fed it to the big man who took it with a smile, swished it round with his pizza, got a few laughs.

The situation, Paul explained, was: Kirby was not only going to be buried in rocks. He was going to be buried in his birthday suit. The rest of the team objected and said it was good enough to bury him in rocks. Bul Paul demanded it, and met their resistance by pushing harder. He got to work.

Having no shovel, and no real method to his madness, he used a combination of bare hands and shirt to dig a hole big enough for the big guy to fit into. He recruited Sam, Dave, and Tyson to help dig the hole, but the last one digging was Paul. The team was half-drunk, half on a second wind, and half-slap happy. When the hole was dug and that time came, Paul clapped and said, Alright big boy, drop the drawers and get in. Kirby came forward, hung his head. The drawers dropped and the ghostwhite flanks flashed in the moonlight.

After finding a hesitant sitting position, he cupped his man parts for protection and sat down and the same guys began to bury him up to his neck. The stones were frigid, heavy, and sharp. Kirby closed his eyes and puffed his breath repeatedly to endure it. On the outside of the circle a little red phone light blinked. They worked until their shirts had stretched to the point of destruction. Then they took a breather.

Paul mounted the big pile where Kirby's head popped out of the top, in a grimace.

Get me outta here! he shouted. I can barely breathe. He struggled to free himself but it was no use.

Paul poured another splash of liquor and tempted it up to Kirby's lips but Kirby spat it away. The fuck is wrong with you, he said. Get me out!

Paul, let's get him out, Sam said, That's good enough. He came forward, but Paul stepped down and barred him from getting closer.

No, it's not good enough. Why is everybody being so soft? It's just rocks, and he's fine. He'll get out soon enough. Alright, he said to the man buried in the rocks, Are you ready for part two? We're just getting started.

Paul came down and unscrewed a blue nalgene water bottle. He looked at Dave and said, Sock, and called with his fingers.

Sock? What for?

Don't worry what for, just give it.

Reluctantly Dave pulled a sweaty sock off his foot and handed it to Paul. As Paul climbed the rock pile he stretched the sock over the mouth of the water bottle and said to the head popping out of the rocks, You know what's coming, don't you?

He gave it a dramatic swirl and lifted the beverage on high for all to see. It's a home brew, Kirby.

Oh hell no, I'm not drinking that shit, get me out get me out of here right now!!

From the top of the pile, Paul saw Felix in his periphery, watching silently from the back, his quiet eyes taking it all in. Then Paul had a better idea. He crouched down with an evil smile on his face, and said Don't worry buddy, I won't make you drink it. He will, and pointed straight through the line of bodies at Felix.

Get up here Felix, it's your turn. If you're going to be part of this team, you gotta earn it. Apparently, all you have to do these days is show up and say I'm here, but on this team that won't cut it. If you're going to run with us you got to play with us too. Get up here now.

Oh come on, Paul, Dave said, Don't make it him. He just got here.

The other guys agreed. Tyson said, Why don't we just be done and do our primal scream? Don't make him…

But no one made him do anything. Felix came forward on his own. Paul was surprised. The evil grin on his face melted to a weak puttylike smile. He staggered to make room on the rocks. Then he handed him the bottle of rank concoction. He said, Now make him drink it, and pointed his toe at Kirby.

Felix drew back instinctively. It was so nasty.

I can't, he said, putting his hand out for Paul to take it back. Paul put his hands in the air.

Felix began to tip it over to spill it, but Paul snatched him by the wrist.

What are you afraid of, Felix? That Mr. Kirby here can't handle this beautiful, beautiful runners cocktail provided by none other than crazy Dave himself? Oh, but you can pull up in your car and just show up halfway through the season and decide you're part of the team? Huh, is that it?

Fine, Felix said. He took the bottle back. With his mild, narrow eyes on Paul the whole time, he brought the bottle near Kirby's shut mouth and shaking head.

Paul began to smile. Everything was bending his way. But then something else happened.

Right as he was about to tip the bottle toward Kirby's face, Felix stood and threw back the bottle himself. The wretched water ran over the sides of his mouth and he gagged, but he gagged it down. He drank it to the dregs with a straight face, and when he was done he threw the empty bottle to the base of the rock pile and hopped down himself. The stunned team parted as he stumbled off into the dark, to the base of a pine tree where he dry heaved and coughed up long stringy pieces of phlegm, tearing it off his lips with two fingers and remain doubled over, his face pale and not a sound coming from him but gags and dead air.

Kirby looked on, disgusted but astonished at this poor kid who did not even know a soul. Paul would not be upstaged by this grand act of rebellion. He made a great chuckling laugh, pretending like it did not phase him, like it did not infuriate him, bound off the top of the rock heap. With a hand outstretched he pulled Kirby out of his dusty tomb, and the kid came out shivering and quivering, with stones falling from every nook.

A few guys came over to Felix and he put his hand up to assure them he was ok.

All right, Paul said, moving right along, completely ignoring Felix in the dark still yakking.

The next part we all know by now, he said. It's a team tradition. A tradition like none other. Come on, it's time for primal scream.

Primal scream was a streak along the beach, followed by a plunge. They did it every year. They followed Paul to the gap in the trees to the dark stony beach. The sand was gritty and smooth stones clacked under their feet.

Clothes off, he said.

They made a pile of their grass-stained shoes and stretched shirts. No one spoke. In years past the streak was always a jolly affair. When they undressed they told dirty jokes, they yipped and snipped and threw sand. But tonight they were solemn. They undressed in silence and stood shivering in the cold, waiting for orders and looking back into the woods, to see if Felix came.

They were still stunned by what happened back there. Momo sat down. He lifted his short up his knee and checked his wound. It looked worse. He said, I'm staying back.

Paul said, Your choice. But grinders find a way.

Dave came up to Paul and said, Are you going to check on Felix?

FELIX, NALGENE, PRIMAL SCREAM

Paul cried out into the dark, Are you coming or not? Are you done being a hero and ready to come play by some rules?

No answer. He shook his head. The team stood waiting in a shivering mass. Tits was about to go get him when Felix appeared in the gap. He made his way over to them and stood among them, fully clothed.

He said it in a calm voice and there was no malice in his eyes.

What are we doing, he asked.

Primal scream, Tits said. We streak the beach and then we plunge.

Felix said, I'll run with you, but I'm not streaking.

You're either all in or all out, Paul said.

Felix smiled, pointed up to the woods. I just..., he started to say, then he stopped. You know what, never mind, I'll sit this one out.

Paul made a careless laugh. Suit yourself, he said. You can stay here with poor Momo and watch if you want or you can head back and go to the cabin and play some cards. Come on boys.

Paul marched them toward the breakers. The rest of them, for tradition's sake, tried to get into the spirit of it. They kicked water at each other and made some animal calls, but it was tame. The run too was tame, not the carefree, balls loose affair it was in years past. Paul could feel the tense legs behind him and he tried to shake it loose by leading a full out sprint at the end. They went for it. Meat flapped and arms flapped. A small ripple of laughter passed among them. Paul veered off into the freezing dumb water and the others followed.

The water was cold and bracing. Goosebumps. Stolen breaths. High girly screams. On all of them but Paul it had a cleansing, purgative effect. They jiggled out of the water, arms tucked, laughing, to check on the other guys. Paul came last. He stayed in the cold water for a long time, hoping others took notice. It was like he was hazing himself, defying the team by tempting hypothermia. He emerged from the frigid vault like a dripping knife. He was blue lipped, livid. The team walked ahead to the cabin and he paced behind, saying not a word to anyone the rest of the night.

Momo ran a high fever that night and Tits nursed him. All night the wound ached and he wheezed because he could not sleep, and the other guys could not sleep because he wheezed. Paul moved his sleeping bag to the main floor and stared up for an hour at the beams and rafters, trying to put away the day by forcing his eyelids down.

He awoke early the next morning with a hangover and sat on the porch. He sipped a cold cup of coffee left over from the day before. It was still dark. The house was asleep. Fog descended. In the distance he heard a far-off snapping in the woods. The sound got closer. Deer, he thought. Wild stags. He heartened at the thought. Every retreat since his freshman year he had seen a shy pair of white tails and antlers skipping through the woods and considered them good luck. He got up and walked to the quiet road and listened and watched. His eyes scanned the woods but he saw nothing and the sound seemed to disappear in his presence. He turned back. When he was close to the cabin, he heard another sound at his back, like the snapping, but different. It had a thump to it, a pulse. Over his shoulder he caught a flicker of orange flying through the fog and a pair of hind legs, smooth as smoke. But that was no deer.

One second was all he caught, but it was sufficient. On

the steps Paul put his throbbing head in his hand and played pretend. He.pretended he did not know who it was who he saw. He pretended he did not have butterflies. He pretended the coffee was not bitter, not cold. He pretended he could not hear the sound of snapping whispering away up the trail. All this he could pretend, and no one ever know.

But when the bell tolled it struck him like a blow.

New coach

They came back that Sunday afternoon, more tired when they returned than when they had left. The next day the new coach was set to make his first appearance. For practice they ran an easy three miler from the high school to the middle school and back. When they arrived back they jogged on the turf then came up through the cafeteria, pushing all the long tables aside and forming a circle on the brown shiny floor where they could do their ab work.

Sam, Dave, and Paul were in the middle of the circle calling time.

Halfway through the workout Sam Bush looked up from a plank and saw the athletic director Mike Nichols waving at him across the room. Next to Mike was someone he had never seen, the new coach presumably. He was a slight man, medium height, with dark wavy hair and a chin that stuck forward.

Sam came over and Mike said, I want to introduce you to the new stand in cross country coach, Cal Brennan. Coach Brennan just got in a few days ago from Washington State and we wanted to introduce himself to you guys as soon as possible.

David Jones joined Sam. The two of them shook hands with the coach. Coach Brennan had a firm handshake and a friendly voice. He looked the two young men in their eyes and asked them how their practice was. He seemed easy going, unobtrusive, about as mild as the sun beaten ball cap he wore.

After the workout the team showed him the locker room and he introduced himself. He told them he had been a runner himself, that he taught sports medicine, and that he was most recently an assistant track coach at East Washington University for 3 years, and was looking forward to a good rest of the season. He had a few boilerplate details about practice times and expectations and upcoming meets. The boys nodded. They sat around the benches in a horseshoe examining the new man.

After he had finished his boilerplate information, he clicked his clipboard against his leg and said, I was sad to hear of Coach Presses departure. I can imagine what he meant to this program and to many of you individually. I know some of you think this season is shot in the foot already. I don't. We might be quarter ways through, but I intend for us to stay strong the next couple meets and hopefully stand in a good position to take counties by the end. We have plenty of talent. Talent won't be our challenge. Focus will. Keeping our eyes and heads ahead of us, on the next race. The time will go quickly. We're going to run hard, but we're going to use our heads too. I'm here to help each of you hit your PR's and then some. My ways aren't the same as coach presses, but that'll be true of every coach you have. We're going to do some different things - take some new measurements, hopefully get you a couple new tricks up your sleeve for race day.

He clicked the clipboard again, then he called roster for the first time. Before he reached the end, he smirked at a little note on the paper he read from. He looked up. Which one of you is Slobbers?

Most of the team laughed in good humor, but Paul said harshly, Don't call me that. Where'd you get that?

Coach Cal said, Excuse me?

Paul said, Don't call me that. It's a nickname you don't have the right to use. I'm Paul to you.

The locker room got quiet. Someone creaked on a bench. Coach Cal nodded and went back to the list. Before he read another name, Paul raised his rude voice again.

So when are we going to hear about Coach Press?

Coach Cal said, We're not. We're not going there. We're going forward.

Why not? Paul insisted. Why can't you say? He kicked his heel into the locker behind him. Why does everyone in this stupid athletic department treat us like we're five years old? So why can't you say?

I can say, but I've been asked not to. And I'm honoring that request. It wouldn't serve the team well...

Paul shook his head. Bunch of bullshit, he griped. If you don't want to be transparent, have it your way, but keep all your tricks up your own sleeve. Without warning he got up to leave. He took his phone from his pocket and rattled it in the air. He said. Sorry Mr. Brennan, I got to take this call. It's from a *real* coach. At Oregon. Where I'm running next year.

Then he shoved out.

Soft hand off

It was a rough start for Coach Cal. When the team left he went back to the office that was once Bill Presses and sat down. He took his hat off and set it on the desk. Then he pulled out the schedule and made notes along the margin and ran through the roster in his mind, trying to remember names and faces. He drew a big X through the name Slobbers.

As he was writing, Momo dropped by. Momo apologized for the confrontation in the locker room. Coach Cal waved and said, Don't worry about it. Every team's got its soap operas. I'll take a soap opera as long as we can drop it when we hit the course. What else can I do for you? he said.

Momo said he'd have to sit out the next couple weeks.

What's going on, Coach said.

Momo lifted his shorts above his knee and showed the bandage and blistered edge of the wound.

It looks ugly, Coach said.

It looks ugly, and it feels ugly, Momo said.

When did this happen?

This past weekend.

On your guy's retreat?

Yeah, Momo sighed. Not pretty.

The retreat or the leg?

Momo smiled. Both.

Do I want to hear about it? Cal pointed to the leg.

You don't want to hear about it.

Fair enough. Coach Cal called his leg over and pulled the bandage down some. He grimaced. He said, I suggest you change out the bandaging every couple hours and keep ice on it as much as possible. It's not deep but it looks infected. Lots of Neosporin. Antibacterial spray. All that stuff. And take it easy. Don't try to force it to heal.

Momo chuckled.

What is it? Coach asked.

You saying, don't force it to heal. If this happened with Press, I'd have dropped the team before I showed him the wound.

Why's that?

He'd just tell me to suck it up and get out there. Anyway, thanks Coach, I'll still be at practice though. Felix can take the number 7 spot for the meets.

Yeah, we'll figure all that out. Thanks for coming by.

Before Momo left, Coach Cal said, Is there anything else I should know about the guys? You all seem a little on edge.

I wouldn't say a little. You got a taste of this already, but watch out for Paul.

I figured. Is he always like that?

No, but ever since Press left, Paul's been going down a bad road. Getting more aggressive. Sniping at us.

Well hopefully it cools down as we get back into it. Thanks for letting me know, Momo.

Momo left and Coach Cal went back to his papers and notetaking. From the drawer he pulled out a manilla folder with 'Soft handoff' written in black marker across the front of it. Inside were a few loose sheets of note paper with Coach

Presses messy scrawl all over it.

Most of the pages were unreadable, but a few toward the back were neater, like he had made an effort to write down something meaningful. It was a list of the runner's names with scraps of notes, physical descriptions, and race times beside it. Coach Cal skimmed along, comparing the notes with the faces he saw in the locker room.

Sam Bush...strong build, good kid, good work ethic, student of the game, strong runner all around...no trouble...

Dave...lazy dave, shaggy hair, crunchy kid, vermonter, birkenstocks, solid kick, easy going, easy strides. can book it once in a while, a top runner.

Tits...sweet kid, tries hard to keep up, puffs his cheeks, chicken legs and a sturdy gut, good lungs (from swimming) but lots of heart, encourager to the team, great pusher, in race and out....

Kirby...big kid, sleeping dragon, mostly sleeping...big chuckle, takes it on the chin, seven older brothers and he's the youngest and tallest... the squirt...poor self image, but consistent, tries, really tries, ties his shoes overtight (why?) ...has potential, but sleeper. one day could blow... possibly...

Tyson...runner in a football player's body, gifted, but no juice, no work ethic, lazy and loveable...dads a gravedigger...wide shoulders... middle pack runner, could be more if wanted to...

Momo...Fiery mexican, speaks spanish when frustrated...speedy but not strong, outmuscled often, fine pusher, complainer, whiner...

makes the team laugh...

When he came to Paul's name, he stopped. There was an empty space and an arrow pointing to the back of the page. He flipped the page, but it was blank. He riffled among the papers but found nothing. Then he stacked the pages and put them away.

Practice

From that day on, Paul never referred to Coach Cal as Coach, but always Cal, or Mr. Brennan. To his team mates he dubbed him The Cardboard Coach. The Standin. Plain Vanilla. Coach Cal was soft spoken and Paul associated this with an evident lack of intensity. The opposite of Press. Coach Cal had a science background and he used words and phrases at practice like 'stroke volume, enlarging capillaries, pronation, VO2 Max.' and others that made Paul yawn.

He also ran with the boys. Usually the runs were full of antics and gossip, but Coach's presence wicked all nonsense and they ran sober. That first practice, Coach Cal ran in the middle of the pack, observing who took the lead and who lingered. Sam and Dave took the lead, and Paul, like an act of defiance, sat in the very back and hummed a mindless tune. They ran seven miles and returned and did a core workout on the track.

Afterwards Coach Cal gave the team a primer on visualization and mental rehearsal. He told the guys to relax and lay down and shut their eyes. He painted a scene of the upcoming race day and told them to try and imagine it as much as they could. In the middle of the exercise, Paul sat up in the middle with his eyes open. He grabbed his water jug from the team pile and unscrewed the lid and swallowed a mouthful of ice. He chewed and spat and smiled down at his teammates.

Coach Cal paused the exercise. He said, Paul, are you here to participate or mock? Paul swung his jug up to his mouth and took a long drink. He wiped his mouth with his hand and said, Neither. I'm here to leave. He looked down at his teammates and shook his head pitifuly I'll leave you little fairies to it. Have fun dreamin, boys.

Then he was gone.

The next day, they did a short five miler, then Coach took slow motion videos of each runner for stride analysis. When it was Paul's turn, he laughed the whole thing off. He said, you want a video of me running you can go on Youtube and watch highlights of the Nike Cross Nationals. Now where do you want me. He hiked his shorts high to his belly button and knotted his shirt in front daisy duke style. He made a farce of it, running like a ditz, like a lady in heels.

Cal knew what he was doing and was not surprised by it. Again he asked Paul, do you want to participate or do you want to mock? Paul said, Neither. I want to run and I want this team to run, not pick our noses and sit around listening to psychobabble.

Later that day, when practice wrapped, Paul called a secret practice over the team group chat. He said, Cal's got a stick up his ass. Tired of soft five milers? If any one's interested in a *real* practice, meet me at the hills at Dempsey park in thirty mins.

No one took him up on his offer. Up and down for the next hour he punished himself on the lonely hills and afterwards took a picture of himself doing another ab circuit and sent it to the group with the text, Only one not pussying out...

He waited a few minutes for a response. Sam wrote back, Lol...well done. Dave wrote back: Grinders find a way. Tyson sent the handclap emoji.

Then, a few minutes later an unknown number popped up on the chat with a picture of a purple bubble tea drink. The text read, Glad you work hard, but sorry, got busy :)

Glad you work hard...Smiley face, Paul thought. Felix... Fucking Felix with his fucking smiley face and purple pussy drink.

Team dinner

They say girls bully with backbiting and boys by brawling, but Paul Stafford, when he got mean, did both.

Paul reread the last message about six more times before the next day. Each time he read it, it infuriated him. He could hear the snideness in it, the punkshit voice of the kid who thought he could waltz on to the team, do nothing and get by.

That night they had team dinner for the race the following day. They ate at a place called the Seafood House, a Chinese buffet on a strip mall in town. Team dinners were optional but it was expected that if you were on the team you showed.

Paul sat at the head of the table. As guys arrived and went to get their food, he noticed the open seat at the table that remained open all dinner. Felix was missing. At first he did not mind. He preferred the original squad and no outsiders. But his eyes floated incessantly to the empty seat, drawn like a magnet. Every time he saw it the voice in his mind repeated the stupid little text with the stupid little smiley face from the day before. *Glad you work hard…*

Paul asked if anyone knew where he was but no one knew. When they were through eating, Paul slumped back in his chair, wiped his mouth on a napkin and threw the napkin across the table, to provoke attention.

The table quieted. He cleared his throat. The team looked up, expecting him to say something, but he kept them in suspense. Folding one hand into his armpit, he held a toothpick with the other, moving it lazily up and down his top set of teeth. He glanced around the table and past it, past all his teammates at nothing in particular. None could read the dark grin on his face. Momo and Tits were at the far end of the table polishing off dessert. They were the only ones not waiting for Paul to speak. They were talking, but not loudly. At last Paul opened his mouth.

Tits, he said, pointing his toothpick out, I see you're back for more.

Tits looked up from his small dish of ice cream. He raised his spoon in the air and smiled broadly at the rest of the table in that lovable, deprecating way he had with his teammates. He was the rubber ball of the team. The one who, 9 times our 10, could take a joke and smile it off and keep rolling. The name, Tits, which he had earned freshman year, was the very declaration of that fact.

A little chuckle went round and circled back to Paul, who appeared to have something more on his mind. But seeing that his first comment found favor, he pursued it.

He said, addressing the table, I never see Tits move as quickly as he does when we come here for team dinner. He might suck at real intervals, but when he comes here, he gives it his all, going between the table and the ice cream machine.

Tits made another spoon nod, another smile across the table, got a few laughs.

Now that Paul secured their attention, he leaned toward the table. Whirled his toothpick.

What'd you go with this time? Halfsies? Half vanilla, half chocolate? Of course you would, Tits.

Paul leaned back. He turned his head, looking around the restaurant, and when he turned back his tone darkened.

Speaking of, he said, where's that other halfsie? Anybody seen him? His eyes poked around the table. He made a play frown, raised his eyebrows. Huh, I guess he's not coming then. And you'd have thought he'd be all over it too, all this good spread. You'd have thought it'd make him feel right at home. He could eat as much of his people's food as he wanted.

As he spoke, he laid eyes on Tits, whose expression had flattened from its happy go lucky smile to a straight face. Tits looked down, then back at Paul. He shook his head and made a small motion with his spoon that said, Cut it out. But the more he motioned for Paul to stop, the more Paul pushed and did not want to be resisted. The reaction gave him energy.

What Tits? You got something to say over there? That's fine if you do, but don't let me interrupt your ice cream eating. Heaven forbid, he declared, putting his hand on his chest. Heaven forbid, as team captain, I should say something at our team dinner about the state of our team. Oh no, but you're over there giving me that little signal, is it? Wanting me to be all pleasant, wanting me to keep my hands in my lap and my mouth shut about halfsies who don't show up, even for team dinner, even before the night of a race. Huh? Is that what you want from me, Tits, with those eyes you're giving me?

The spoon snapped against the table. There was a moment of hesitation as the team looked from side to side. To say that Tits did not ordinarily punch back or get into spats with other people, was an understatement. He did not ever. But all at once, he said firmly, Shut up Paul.

Tits was done eating, done smiling, done letting Paul spitball whatever he wanted to spitball. Paul could see the change come over him, but instead of toning down, he toned up.

What Titsy, you got something to say with what I said?

Yeah, shut up. You're being offensive. Stop talking about him like that.

Talking about whooo? Paul made a bantering little 'o' with his lips and gave a look to Dave and Sam, trying to pull them into his scheme.

Are you serious right now? Tits said. Do you think we're dumb?

Yes, I'm serious. Unless you can talk better for me than I can... I'm not the one around here twisting any words. I'm just asking questions. Plain questions. Straight questions...

He was playing him, cat and mouse like, Paul the cat and Tits the mouse.

Why are you so offended anyway? Why don't you go back to that bowl of sugar you got waiting for you, champ? Besides, I'm not saying anything offensive.

Not to you, Tits returned.

What, you're offended? Paul laughed. At me just joking around some about our no show?

Our 'no show'? Dude, do you hear yourself?

I'm not saying anything but stating a fact as obvious as the size your man-Tits are going to be by the time you're finished with all that ice cream, he laughed. He was the only one laughing.

You're talking about Felix, right? He's the one you're calling the no show and the halfsie?

Paul smiled. He set his pick down and placed his two pointers on the edge of the table, tapping them back and forth, back and forth, waiting for Tits to come at him again.

Tits said, You should at least have the courtesy to call him your teammate. Instead of trashing him behind his back.

Paul removed his fingers from the table and chuckled, No, I will not call him my teammate, because as far as the rules go, which I read for clarification the other day, all rosters must be set by the end of tryouts. Which is long gone by now. That's the rules. I didn't make them up, but they're set in stone, and I, unlike you, have the decency to say I follow the rules like a man. No matter how much Mike Nichols, our stupid AD says he's all about inclusion and waving his hands around saying anybody can join whenever they like. He's a tool. And no matter how much you wanna stomp your foot and raise your voice, he's officially not on the team, according to the rules. He's a Hawaiian shirt wearing, no show, halfsie. And halfsie's the only right name you can give to a kid like that. All he is is half. Half in, half out, half runner, half whatever else he does.

A bit of foam had gathered at the edge of Paul's lip. He wiped his mouth with the back of his hand. His indignant eyes did a lap around the table to see who was taking his side against Tits.

With the exception of Momo, the rest were not looking up, but down. Tyson and Kirby looked embarrassed, but Dave and Sam wore the kind of cowardly, weak smile young men wear when they're content to sip on shameful speech rather than speak up against it.

Is that all, Tits? Titsy? Paul concluded. Anyone else? Anyone else you want to go around the circle with and do your girl scout affirmations? Anyone else's feelings I hurt by speaking the truth?

Tits said, So if he's not really on the team then his times

won't count? According to the rules...

Shut up, Tits. What I'm saying is that whoever wants to pansy out can pansy out. Just like cardboard coach, just like Mike Nichols. What I am saying is that I, me, and whoever else has the balls to follow the rules and what the rules say, won't count them. He can run, sure, but up here he said, tapping his temple, there will be no real times. Only a big fat asterisk, one after another.

Then he jumped back at Tits.

You know what Tits? Instead of you getting up all up in arms, why don't you just sit back there and enjoy your ice cream and let the big boys talk for a moment. Go back to your little kid's table. Eat your fortune cookie. Figure out if it tells you how you can stop being so slow and actually help your team in races, instead of being every year of high school at the back of the pack, the pusher of pushers, the weekend warrior. OK? Sound good? Go figure that out, then talk. Go on and break a couple school records, then a couple county and state records, then earn yourself a scholarship to Oregon and actually do something with the – I won't call it talent – but whatever it is you've got - instead of running your trap against me, running your trap behind people's back, because you got nothing better to do. You know what, don't even worry about showing up tomorrow. Leave your bib on the bus. Just tell Mister cardboard coach you pulled a muscle or something with all that overtraining you're doing. Although it clearly hasn't been working for your man-Tits. I'm glad we still get to call you that. You were Tits then and you're Tits now. And I imagine with the phenomenal work ethic you've got, you'll be a good old Tits five years from now when you're a lonely virgin whacking off in your dorm room and not out running because you didn't have the balls to go out for the team.

To show that he was through making a fool of him, Paul picked up his napkin from the center of the table and threw it down at him with a cruel, scoffing laugh that left the table in a gloom. It was a shame to hear. A shame to all of them, but to Tits foremost, who felt so belittled, so unspeakably full of rage he could not move, but only stare straight ahead, his mouth open, and his short breath going in and out past his dry lips.

When the abuse ended he broke his stare and rose from the table, grabbing his bag from below. He pushed his chair in and made his way to the door.

Hey, first pay up! Paul shouted at his back. Tits stopped. He turned over his shoulder. There was no such thing as a separate bill for team dinner. There was a single meal and a single bill.

I thought…

You thought what? You're eating on the house? Nope.

Before it got any worse, Momo cut in, Guys, quit it.

But Paul wouldn't have it. Shut up you too, Momo. Unless you want out like Tits and you can throw in whatever pesos you've got there too. If you've got them.

With a hard shove Momo was up without a moment's deliberation. He took his wallet and threw down thirty bucks for him and Tits.

Tits walked to the door and Momo followed, limping some. Before they left, Momo turned with a sad face and said to Paul, What happened to you man? Then they were gone, leaving the other five with stones in the pits of their stomach and nothing more to say.

Meet

The rift between them grew. Since retreat they had felt it in the stifled laughter and mean joking and drunken bouts. But now it was something visible, something tangible and fearsome.

The day of the meet, Tits arrived at the bus dressed in street clothes. He carried no duffle, no spikes, singlet, or bib. He wore headphones and the same expression on his face he had the night before. He hardly said anything to anyone all bus ride long. The only person he said a word to was Momo. He whispered something that drifted from the front of the bus to the very back where Paul sat in the middle between Sam and Dave. His elbows were on his knees and his hand dipped in and out of a bag of ranch flavored sunflower seeds. He glowered down the aisle, saw the whisper pass from one treacherous set of lips to the next.

The bus rumbled on, through interstate and county roads. There were dozens of empty seats in the middle and a clear unmistakable hierarchy. The underclassman and the slower runners sat toward the front, and the upperclassmen and the fast boys sat in the back. It was like all school buses in a way.

Coach Cal rode separately, but in the days before, it was customary for Coach Press to ride with them on race day. He used to get up halfway through the ride, fold his composition book in half and whack it against his leg as he gave them a pep talk for the race. His big barking presence filled the bus. He would stand at the very front, and as his passion grew, his eyes would sweep from front to back, lingering on each of his runners not more than a second before ending and resting on Paul, who always got a wink.

The Pretty Eyes, Dave called that look. One time when they were stretching on the course before the race, Dave nudged Paul and said, Hey Paul, if you don't break your old record today after Press was giving you the pretty eyes all bus ride long, I think he might dock you a couple extra months after you graduate before you can finally date his daughter.

What are you talking about? What pretty eyes?

Oh! As if you don't know. I'm talking about how every bus ride, before Press claps his hands and tells us to go get em', he gives you a three second stare and a wink, because you're his golden boy. *The pretty eyes.*

But that afternoon there was no Press, no pretty eyes. Paul's mind fell to contemplating the secret passed from Tits to Momo. He chewed and spat, chewed and spat his sunflower seeds and his concentration wrote a line down the middle of his forehead. He thought of last evening. He was certain they were talking about him and what happened at the restaurant.

He rolled his crinkly bag shut, stood and raised his voice. All right girls, second half of the season starts now. Time to cut the flab and run like stags for once. I think we've had enough girl gossip about Presses departure, but I think it's time we run like he was there with his bucket at the finish line. I got my sights on a pr today, to inch us closer to county champs. So for every one of you *real* stags, who's dressed and ready to go – the rule is: 'balls to the wall' and 'run like someone's chasing you' (both Press-isms)

Hoorah, Sam cheered. Dave pounded the back of the seat before him. Tyson smiled. The rest of the team heard the message and faced forward. They unloaded the gear from the back of the bus and made their tent. Coach Cal was there already flipping through his roster and talking with the other coaches. He pulled the team together and offered a few remarks about giving it a good effort and finishing strong. Then it was time. Bibs, warmups, hydration, butterflies. Last minute pees. Tape on blisters. A crowd of colors, glossy shorts slit up the side, floppy haircuts. A trickle of fans. Piles of backpacks, water jugs. Numbers, naked shoulders, hairy thighs.

Starting line. Then the gun.

Like the stroke of a brush the pack was off, the ground apatter with jittery footstrikes. Level heads and initial bursts and easy arm carriage. Within a hundred yards of the starting line you had pushers and pacers and stragglers from Mayo high.

Paul was near the front, with Sam and Dave close behind. Tyson and Kirby were middle of the pack. Felix was right behind them, coasting along the fringe. The first mile of the race he stayed at the fringe, jostling here and there with a few strivers from the back of the pack and a few of the pacers who lost steam.

The race was called Gideon Forge, or just, The Forge. It was a middle of the road course with a mile or so that ran through a stand of woods, both on the first half when the course sloped down for the most part, and again on the second when the winding trailing climbed up. Press used to call courses like this 'good ol down and uppers'

The name Gideon took from a stone building that marked the halfway point. It was an abandoned farmhouse of some kind that had fallen into disrepair and had looked like that for twenty years. The wide path converged to a singular, almost single file patch of hard packed mud where the trail doglegged steep to the left and the runners fanned out again. The sky was a deep shock of blue and big lobes of clouds swept across the sky. Trees shook and branches quaked from the wind, which was wild and batting and added a thrill of refreshment to the competition.

At the dogleg, Paul was neck to neck with his own PR. He was well ahead of the nearest runner, which was Sam Bush, who trailed him comfortably by twenty seconds, and Sam was another twenty seconds ahead of his nearest competitor.

The cold wind was at their backs and it continued riding up and up as they drove ahead, keeping their good form. Both sets of eyes looked straight ahead and neither looked back to see who, if any, attempted to close the distance. Behind them, in the mush of the pack, Kirby tousled with Tyson and plowed through a chain of runners from Riverdale in blue and gold singlets and made a seam for Felix who had drifted all that time like a wind carried cloud to join their ranks. Kirby yelled in his deep voice, Get over here, Felix! And Felix came and entered the mush with his teammates. A smile broke across his face. He was tentative at first, but he picked up speed and took courage. There you go! Kirby said.

Then it was Kirby, Tyson, and Felix, moving together. Not too far off, Dave Jones started up a ridge where nettles and brush encroached on the path. Dave was losing steam. His stride was slipping and he was caught in a knot of speedsters from Central high.

Through waves of runners, through wheeling arms and clods of earth flung from back heels, each of the stags could see one another like links in a chain of red, all the way up to Paul, who continued to muscle ahead like an ox with hind legs, his head down and his arms going up and down without variation or interruption.

Kirby kept pushing, grunting and driving and grunting some more. Tyson began to lag, saying under his breath, Son of a b, son of a b! Kirby looked back and threw him a dirty look.

The hell did I do? Kirby yipped at him, out of breath.

Not you, him! Tyson said. He threw his glance up ahead at Felix, who with two flashing strides overtook them and passed on the left. There was no build up. It was a swift surge. Kirby was so stunned by the ease with which he passed he began to lag as he watched the new guy float up ahead, moving across the course like a shadow. His carriage was easy. His foot strikes were soft and graceful.

Well shit…Kirby said. They watched him go. Momo, watching from the team tent, saw the move and said something similar in Spanish. As he streamed by, Felix looked back with hesitation, as though he were afraid of parting with his comrades, but they threw their hands at him and harassed him, Go! go! go! Get the hell out of here!

He moved, alright. Though move is a word that did not do justice to the way he covered the ground. He was like silk through a magician's hands, like the clouds that soared overhead. A lean, arrowing shadow, without temper, panic, pulsing veins or clenched fists. He ran the way a sailboat swings through the sea.

Up he went past the loud Dominion boys, past lazy Dave,

even past Pete Walker from Centreville, the only other in-county runner who gave Paul a scare once or twice a year. In a mile he chewed through a meaty pack and faced the last half mile bend through a patch of woods, then the straightaway.

Paul ran in a silo of his own excellence. Sam grit his teeth and pounded through his screaming lungs. He pushed and pushed, forced his body machine along as it delivered a fine performance. And then there was Felix. Felix, who seemed at the last leg of the race to be just beginning. Felix, whose last name no one knew, who was an enigma, who had slipped his way onto this tumultuous team during this most tumultuous season. Felix, who had lagged all race long, and who, from one word of encouragement, took off, ripped the last quarter mile to ribbons and nearly caught Sam Bush in the process. He crossed the finish line in third, and came into the chute looking like he still had gas in the tank.

Gradually the drove of other runners flowed in and flowed out with the commotion of coaches and local sports reporters and coaches and spectators. Felix's feat flowed out with the commotion. By two and a half seconds Paul snapped his old course record and Sam PR'd.

Coach Cal called the team together after everyone had finished and gave the top finishers a place in a huddle, a circle of applause to commend their excellent performance. As the applause died, a kind of hush replaced the congratulations. Coach said, Those aren't the only performances we have to acknowledge, is it? He looked around. No one came forward immediately. No one wanted to be the first to steal Paul's course record spotlight, but it was Tits again who came forward.

These guys ran a good race, no doubt, but I want to

acknowledge Felix, who finished third and absolutely cleaned up the last mile and a half in spite of stiff competition.

Kirby started a clap and slowly it picked up and petered out, but mostly Felix got stunned looks. Really? Third? Did he say that right?

Felix was modest. He did not bask under the spotlight or say much. He nodded to those who nodded at him. Paul, quick to cut it off though, said to Tits, I guess the competition was too stiff for you, apparently. Are you assistant coach, giving your post-game analysis in jeans? Paul laughed at his own comment, and Tits ignored the comment, then the team dismissed to stretch.

A few minutes later Paul pulled Tits behind the bus and gave him more hell, You have no right to speak. Like back there. If you can't take your tampon out and suit up like a man and get into the pit like the rest of us, you literally cannot talk. Got it? You think you're making some kind of statement not gearing up. Skipping out. You've been talking like you've earned a right to talk. I got news for you – you haven't. Runners run, ok? That's what you're here to do. They don't go pulling out their stupid soap boxes just because they got their feelings hurt.

Paul, what are you talking about?

I know what you're doing.

The hell are you talking about Paul? I didn't say anything to you. I congratulated you. You're losing your shit. I wasn't doing anything but giving credit to…

Paul pushed him in the chest.

I'm not losing my shit. I'm being a captain. Which *I* am and which *you're* not. Meanness shot out of Paul like a six shooter, and Tits stood there taking it, bullet by bullet. I miss the old you, he said, dropping his voice. Paul could raise his voice or lower it, but it was when he spoke lowest that he said the meanest things.

…I miss the gigolo Tits, the Tits sandwich, the Tits that Press let onto the team because he felt bad for you, and *only* because he felt bad for you.

Paul left him on the spot. When he was out of sight, Tits said to himself, Yeah I miss the old you, too.

It was the second big confrontation the two of them had in two days. That alone was a major warning sign for the rest of the team. Tits, as noted before, was the bellwether of the team. The thermometer, telling the team whether it was on good terms with itself or not. Certainly it was not. Even the other teams that lost handedly that race had regrouped and showed no signs of morbidity. But the stags, who came in one, two and three, were stalled. Defeated winners they were.

Standing there post-race, they looked stranded, wilted. The bloom and the struggle and joy of running was gone – replaced by bickering, phone staring, cheap and heartless laughter.

The only two who appeared unshaken by the team mood were the two new guys, Coach Cal and Felix. Coach Cal was aware of the fighting, but he took it as a matter of course and let them have it out on their own. Felix was nonchalant, almost childlike. When Paul and Tits went at it he merely watched, neither affirming or denying or decrying any of the points being made. He put on his breezy hawaiian shirt and thong sandals. When the team was gathering gear to reload the bus, Kirby saw him squatting under a nearby tree tossing crumbs of club crackers to squirrels. He laughed.

There was something unusual about this kid, something that ran against the grain. Later Kirby looked and saw Felix dancing, perhaps? His hands were moving in a funny way. What was that? One hand followed the other in a smooth, electric wave, where the tips of his fingers on one hand appeared connected by a magnet on the other. It was a curious thing to see. Kirby did not know what to make of it. He would do it and stop. Do it and stop.

But soon enough, it became clear. A deep bass hip hop beat erupted behind the bus. There was a scuffle, flashes of movement and airborne feet seen below the bus. *Thump-thump diga-diga,* the beat went, *thump-thump diga.*

Momo was closest to the back of the bus. He caught the first glimpse. Then he came around full and said Dammmm son…

It was difficult to describe what kind of dancing it was, with all its fluidity and dynamism. But it was easy to describe what it was not. It was not the YMCA. And it was not the foxtrot. And it was certainly not white people country club wedding dancing. It was *dancing* dancing; some hip hop, b-boy, pesto pop blend, and it was really, really good. His feet bounced smoothly, shifted, cha-cha-ed, and his upper body popped in and out to the beat. During that space of time when more teammates poked their head around to watch him, his arms rolled, one on top of the other, like two electric currents riding through them. All his limbs synchronized to the beat. It was amazing. Felix was so lost in the routine he did not notice Momo standing there until someone spilled the water cooler nearby and the sound broke his concentration.

Felix looked up and pushed the hair off his face where it stuck to his forehead. He had broken another sweat. He aired his shirt.

Dam son, Momo clapped, I feel like my leg's getting better just watching you…why didn't you tell us?

Tell you what? Felix replied, a little bashful but also a little cheeky.

Whatever that was. You can dance, man. What were you doing? Practicing something? And how'd you get those moves?

Felix deflected the praise. He said, It's in the blood. My mother's Dominican, and my father's Korean…

Pshhhh, Momo said, Don't give me that. Dominican, ok. But I've seen a lot of stiff Koreans in my day. You don't just inherit those moves.

Felix didn't want to draw attention to it, so he downplayed it. As he scooped his boombox off the ground, he said, It's something I do to relax. I've been doing it the past couple years. Dancing's my first love.

The rest of the team trickled in by then. Enough to see some, not all the performance. Paul was unimpressed. Sam and Dave did not know what to make of it. Kirby, Tits, and Tyson wanted to see more. They pestered him to do something else, just a taste.

Felix said, Another time we'll do it again, but not just me, all of us.

After that they loaded the bus and found their seats. The whole ride back the pestering continued. Momo said, So do you call that popping and locking? You weren't krumping were you? Or were you? Then he came out and said, You know, I've never told anyone, but I secretly *love* dancing. Like the kind of dancing you do, Felix. Whatever it's called. The kind they have in the movies with the dance battles. I watch that stuff on youtube all the time. I can't dance, but if I could…

You gotta practice, Felix said.

Yeah right…with this gimp…

They made a huddle in the front. Felix lowered his voice at one point, and explained that dancing was one of the reasons he missed last team dinner and would have to miss some of the practices. He was in a hip hop dance troupe that met at Sylvan Heights, their rival high school, since theirs did not have one. He also had special permission from Coach Cal.

I'm trying not to draw too much attention to it, he said.

I'm fine with it, Momo said. I think all of us up here are fine with it. But…

Momo thumbed backwards.

Yeah, Felix said, that's why.

When the huddle broke, Momo went on talking to Felix. No one ever heard Momo so talkative, so genuinely enthusiastic. It was out of character. He was what the team called The Mumbling Mexican, even though technically he was El Salvadorian. That was part of the joke. He was sarcastic and had a dark sense of humor. And he really did mumble, all of his complaints and a good share of dirty jokes.

Here he was, with a face like sunshine, all up in Felix's grill. Hey dude, he said, All I want is for you to teach me a couple of those moves, one of the really simple ones, like nothing too complicated, but still sexy, if you know what I mean. It's gotta be sexy still, cuz we got homecoming soon and once my leg's healed, if it ever heals, I don't want to do any more of that white boy, nasty, bump n grind, sex with clothes on, bullshit they call dancing. That's all they do. Did they do that wherever you were before?

The louder he got the more he stood out of his seat without knowing, and Kirby, who split his attention between the front of the bus and watching the reaction of the back, said Momo, sit down.

Nah, man, you sit down. This is America, and this is a bus, and I'm no Latino Rosa Parks who needs to sit down in my seat. I can stand if I want to. I can dance in my seat if I want to, I can…

He was on a roll, when suddenly he yelled out in pain and grabbed his hurt leg. Something hit him. He turned and saw the culprit projectile skidding down the middle aisle, a full Nalgene bottle, launched from the back. It hit the wound dead on. Momo collapsed on the seat by necessity. His leg pulsed with pain. There was a roar of laughter from the back and Paul yelled out, Now you're the Bleeding Mexican, Momo. Put your head down and stop talking so loud. Some of us here are trying to have a captain's meeting, but all we hear is your yabber yabber.

You never saw vengeance overtake a happy person's face so quickly as it overtook Momo's at that moment, as he hunkered in his seat. Fresh blood oozed out the gauze and down the side of his knee. His right hand was smeared in yellow pus. His nails dug into the seat and his face was near purple with rage. Kirby looked at him. He had never seen him like that.

Momo was about ten seconds from doing something he would regret, when the bus driver spoke up on the intercom and the bus hiccupped to a stop.

Sorry, we're going to be a couple minutes late here. Looks like we've got a pile up, couple ambulances coming from the high school.

And just like that all eyes were on the windows.

Glit

All the evil vibes faded away with concern about what was going on, of who was hurt or what happened. They dropped the windows to the bus and listened in suspense as people went this way and that. A huge crowd of students flooded the staircase outside the main gymnasium. The crowd flowed from the football field. The coaches stood together with their hats off, the cheerleaders with pom poms at their feet stood apart, some of them crying into each other's shoulders.

The bus was stopped at a light and had not moved through three green lights. Finally the crowd began to part. The two large doors to the gym opened and the people crowded on either side of the railings and made a lane. Paramedics and police officers brought one stretcher, then another. That was all they could see from the bus. Then the ambulance packed, the flashing lights started, and sirens filled the air.

By the time they entered the lot, they could hear the names of their classmates, Grayson Allen, and Bryce Cooley, on every post. The two were taken to the hospital on account of a freak collision, or some accident of which at first there was no agreement, and even contradictory testimonies.

Some people appeared to protest. One of the parents from

the opposing team shouted out, I bet this is one of their big old plays. Throw the game when they're down two touchdowns. I didn't see anything happen.

One of the Stag parents fired back. He told the outspoken skeptic he was sick in the head. Go back to your hickville cornfield football field and have some compassion on an injured player.

Injured? the other guy came back. The one guy wasn't even in the game, he was coming onto the field. And don't tell me it was a collision. You tell me the truth when you've seen footage of the play. I've got it right here on my phone because I was videotaping it, and what I saw is a bunch of mamby pamby Mercedes driving fakes. It's a coverup.

A beer bottle flew one way and crashed, then a bottle flew the other way and crashed.

ven when the players in question had been rushed from the school, the parking lot remained jammed with drama. The cross country team picked their bags off the asphalt and waited off to the side. None of them went home, though they were free to go.

There was a group of students waiting at the gym doors. Someone called out, What's everyone waiting for? And someone called back, Mike Nichols is going to come out and offer a statement about what went on, what really happened.

Paul, Sam, and Dave joined a group of other team captains on the stairs, while the underclassmen remained by the sidewalk, checking their phones for any updates across social media.

But word traveled faster than media. A kid named Lance Hughes was making his way down the line of people standing off to the side. He was relaying some message. People were listening to him. Lance was a senior and one of the popular kids in his class, well liked in general. As he went down the line, he skipped the parents and went straight to the students.

He was holding in his hand, opening it and closing it like a secret game of show and tell. When he saw the team standing there waiting, he ran over and, closing his fist first, pointed up at the gym doors.

Don't believe a word, he says. They don't know what's going on. They think they do. Here's a real clue. He put his hand out, made a look that said, Check it out. Felix, Kirby, and Momo leaned in. There was a tiny pink pill lost in the crease of his palm. It sat in a soft powdery substance flecked with glitter. He snapped his hand shut.

You've seen that before?

They shook their heads.

Ever heard of glit?

Glint?

No, Glit. Like glitter.

He rolled his eyes. You guys are cross country right? You guys are the good kids. Never mind then, ask around. You have nothing to worry about.

There were people calling him to come over. As he was walking away, the gym doors opened. Mike Nichols came out flanked on either side by his assistant director and the assistant principal of the school. Before he started talking, Kirby called out to Lance. What's it do?

Lance hushed his voice. He said, Do you remember my namesake, Lance Armstrong? When he went into beast mode.

Kirby said, yeah.

Imagine that, but clean and smooth, no rage, and a high like lovemaking. So I hear. Couple guys found this in their bags and were throwing it out before anyone saw.

Are there side effects then, or was it a collision, or…?

Lance shrugged. He strode off, then turned back and said, You know what I know. By the way, you didn't hear it from me. There might be more of it too. But you guys are good. You're cross country, he smiled. Then he was gone.

Tremors

For a solid week there was a mass amount of media and administration racket about the matter. The AD stuck to his PR guns and told everybody the boys were in good condition. And on the matter of substance abuse, there was no substantial evidence, but that they were looking into the matter further. The principal likewise offered statements affirming the school's longstanding no exception policy about drug use, scholarships, penalties, blah blah.

On ground zero, on the student level, there was a lot of talk about Glit. What it was and what it wasn't. They called it the bubble gum powder with a sparkle. There were memes about it being a viral beauty product, blush for the ladies ahead of homecoming, a combination of Viagra and Adderall. There were jokes about how girls softball could use an extra shipment or two and see how that worked on their record. And still other jokes about how it was the same stuff they squeezed out of bags to make powdered eggs. A lot of hoopla about glit. But a lot of it, or most of it, was speculation and there appeared to be little truth.

At the end of the week, Bryce Cooley came back from his time at home after being borne off the field in a stretcher. He was flocked like a superstar, this big, blockheaded tight end, who was in remedial math and not what you would call a cool kid. Sam Bush knew him and asked him between periods what was up, and Cooley said Nothing's up, but they offered me a butt ton of cash to keep my trap closed, so that's what I'm going to do.

The other guy, Grayson, was no better. People tried to pull something out of these two and none could. Despite being one of the best teams in the whole school for their sport, cross country only received gossip like that second hand. They were never privy to juicy news. None of them but Paul, and occasionally Sam and Dave.

Practice resumed as usual. On Thursday they ran fartleks, on Friday hill repeats, on Saturday a short run. Sunday, rest. On Monday, after practice, the team, at Coach Cal's encouragement appeared for Paul's award reception. He was being given a surprise cross country legacy award, after news of his latest course record. Other athletes from other sports were honored too. They held the ceremony in the main auditorium. Mike Nichols and his two assistants were there. It was the first year they gave away legacy awards, and some thought it was another slick PR move to cover up the rash of scandalous news.

All of this was happening. And all of it appeared on the surface like a matter of course, like a succession of events typical of any high school during any time at any place. On one level that was right. But there was something happening below the surface, tremors that began when Paul took up the yoke of his old coach. The days passed and the tremors did not die. They grew.

Bull Run

The next race was that following Tuesday. Bull Run, one of the toughest runs of the season. The course was infamous in the region for its perilous inclines and declines, for its broken hills and ambling, jagged crests. And for its reputation for hosting some of the best all-out battles in men's cross country. It was a regional meet and frequently an event blue chip college scouts attended for top running talent.

Five years back, when Paul swept counties and states, he had a memorable showdown at Bull Run with Chapelgates then top runner, Milo Dunne. The two were close the whole race, until Paul out-kicked him in the final stretch, and Milo tripped off course into an area roped off for park goers and picnickers. The year after Paul was equally impressive, leading the team on a streak that won counties and regionals. It was one of the races where Bill Press looked like he actually enjoyed coaching, instead of an angry Desert Storm general called to the front.

After that race Coach Press made a few comments to the local paper that became somewhat famous at the school the rest of the year. When asked how he prepared the team for the race, he said, Prepared? We've been prepared for this race all year long. We've been working hills that make these hills look like a flat chested woman next to Dolly Parton. When asked what advice he gave them in the bullpen, he said, I told them no jelly legs, no loser limps, no pulling out early when the bull begins to chase and snort. And I told them, go after the course like a hen at a hobo picnic.

A hen at a hobo picnic. That was the phrase that stuck and made its way through the school and remained in his runner's head like some treasured wisdom, one of his countless sayings he probably stole from someone else.

Press the man was not the only thing missing that day. His fighting spirit, his whole pistol and holster approach was missing. Paul felt it and felt responsible for it. He felt that he must summon, if he could, the wily spirit of his mentor, to gather that loose assemblage of arms and legs and dumb injuries that was his team, and say something to rouse them for the race.

When they got there, they filed out of the bus slack, their heads in a cloud. Kirby had forgotten to pack their pop-up tent, so they roughed it, throwing their bags in a pile by the buses. The starting line overlooked the mean looking, up and down course. Bumps and slashes at every pass. Scrub and brakes and bushy nettles. Below was a stream of water catching light through the trees. Paul took a moment by himself and surveyed the course, calculating his well-known route. For the first time since running that course, he recognized the meaning of what the race organizers called The Bull's Ring, which was the way the creek circled upon itself like a ring. The feature could only be seen from high up, and it was the very point his eyes picked out, the gold gleam of water that lay against the rest of the brown and red, raw-boned land like a stud in the snout of a steer.

He came back to the pile of bags and called a huddle while Coach Cal was talking to one of the other coaches.

He said, Everybody knows Bull Run's a test. Some might even say that it's the test. It shows who's showing up and who isn't, who's trained and who hasn't. Press, if he was here, would have all of us pick up a clod of dust and give it a good rub it between our palms like this, because he knew that to race well you've got to…

Before he finished his statement, he looked up and saw the underclassmen trailing off.

Hey Tits, Felix, he snapped his fingers. Their heads turned. What was I just saying?

Tits, who was dressed to run, smiled and said, Let me guess, You were going to tell us to run like hell and go after the course like it was a hen at a hobo picnic, or something like that, right?

The team laughed, but the weak smile on Paul's face leveled. While Tits was talking, he came right up to him, spat on his shoes and pushed him hard backwards. Dave came and separated them. Let it go Paul. Just let it go. He was joking.

Tits sat on the ground a moment. No, that's his problem. He can't let it go, Tits said. He can't drop his stupid fucking ego enough to just let us run. Put on our jerseys and run. Instead of trying to be Bill Press. You're not Bill Press. You don't need to be going around patrolling all of us, pretending you're a hard ass like he is. Run your own stupid race. And stop thinking the world revolves around you and your running career.

Paul stood erect, coiled, held back the whole time by Dave. His chest puffed in and out quickly. Tits picked himself off the ground with Momo's help and dusted himself off. He flicked a rock off his elbow.

He said sadly, I was joking with you right now, Paul. Couldn't you hear that? Everyone else did. I was giving you a hard time, trying to help you lighten up some.

You weren't joking, Paul grimaced.

I was joking, even if it did rib you a little bit. That's the point of a joke, that it gets to you. But you didn't hear it that way. Everything that touches you breaks, everything that crosses you gets cut, for no purpose, no purpose at all but for you to prove to yourself you're still something without Press blowing bubbles up your ass. It's not what you think.

What's that supposed to mean?

Tits turned aside to Kirby and Kirby gave him a look that said, Don't say.

But Tits was so upset, he went on, What you'll find out eventually is you're not who you thought you were in Press's eyes. You're not some golden child, some one in a million godsend runner, or whatever it was he said to you to get you to take your pants off.

The whistle blew and the huddle broke and the runners gathered at the line. That is how the race started, just short of a meltdown. But when it came time to race, hard words were laid aside, swallowed, stomached.

Feet at the mark.

From the get-go, Paul blew out the gates and tore at the hills, chewing up earth and splitting open his compact stride. It was like the words just spoken to his face were still humming in his ears and he was driving them deaf with speed, fighting them, and fighting himself. His stroke was violent, erratic. He slowed then sped, slowed then sped, but even when he slowed he was fast compared to other runners.

Along the rough turf he pounded. He ran and ran, his breath getting away from him, and his arms which had been so well trained to carry at his side, began to untether, swatting at swaying catclaw and cattail and high grass he cut through. Alone for a while he battled, strode, made record pace while the flies swarmed, and hung and hovered and drifted behind him. Paul, at that point in the race, was not only the *Run* of Bull Run, he was the *Bull*. Even his confreres, Sam and Dave were caught in the turmoil of the pack. But the Bull broke loose, mad and white eyeballed, with a snort that whiffled through his nose every few strides, disrupting his pattern of easy aerobic breaths.

On he went, stampeding, muscling ahead; indomitable bull, raging bull, mean as the mafia, and untouched by the housefly pace. Until something caught his attention. Something at his six. Something that he could feel and smell and hear before he saw. He could not and would not turn his head initially. To do anything like turn back to see if anyone was in his range felt too much like weakness, like doubt.

He began to hear the words he had heard so many times before.

Eyes ahead, eyes ahead. Loosen up the shoulders, tempo, tempo, faster, faster. These were the words he spoke to himself and recycled in his mind. They were not his own words and it was not his own voice, but Press'.

Tempo, tempo, faster, faster, arms loose, eyes soft. The voice grew angrier, like it was no longer a coach making calculations, but a spirit nagging. Eyes soft, eyes soft. But he could feel his eyeballs in his head, the pressure and strain moving like a knot into his temples. Don't look back, don't look back. Eyes ahead. Eyes soft. Move forward. Don't look back. Words and more words, louder and louder. The more they filled his mind, the more his mind divided. He tried to unhear the anger in the voice, yet heed the commands, but he could do neither. Shut up, shut up! he ordered himself.

He ran by instinct, but his instincts were dumb. Words shot at him. Grinders find a way, grinders find a way. Now his head was down and he hit the patch of gravel that marked the last mile of smoking uphill. His overall pace was slowing, and he could feel it slowing. He could feel his pedal to the metal, but the car would not shift, the gear would not turn, and the harder he tried to push the more he felt the needle straining on the dash.

The other runners, the cloud of houseflies, dispersed a half mile back, becoming a tattered rope of twos and threes. But the figure behind Paul, who he had smelled and felt and heard, but had not seen, was still there at his six, and felt so damnably near now. Another gear slipped. He stalled, caught himself, dragged forward, strained forward. The course leveled a final time. There, in the last 400 meters, blind to all features but the finish line, his attention, which he trained forward, now under the influence of his strain, snapped. His bull neck whipped, his heavy eyes launched backward, as if drawn to the approaching fear, and he saw Felix coming. Coming, coming… like a shook cape, like a flash of saber. Unstrained, no snout to the dust. Calm and swift and austere and sudden.

And then it was over.

Paul outlasted him by two measly seconds. He stumbled into the chute dizzy and lightheaded. His feet wandered. His temples pulsed. His spinning head glanced and saw the official times and his stomach turned. He brushed past fellow racers and floating heads of congratulations, past Coach Cal and his outheld fist bump, past the horseshoe of waiting buses, and went on up past the soccer fields to the lonely bathrooms. There he bent over the yellow enamel sink and heaved a pale mush of half-digested crackers down the drain and splashed his face and washed his hands twice with soap. He set his hand on the sink and watched it tremble.

Then he released a fierce, bloodcurdling cry that he had never heard himself make before. His thoughts spun. His heart fluttered. He tried to compose himself, to compose his face and erase the deep furrow that ran the middle of his forehead, but it wrenched into position by habit. He rushed back to camp. In his head he kept calling it 'camp'. Why was he calling it camp? Not one thought could he hold on to and keep. His trembling persisted all the way down. He tripped over a mound of grass as he was coming off the main sidewalk, picked himself up, and slowed down as he reached his team, hoping to slip among them.

Sam and Dave joked with Kirby as they recounted their runs. Tits, who made his flesh creep, was on a foam roller. Momo was talking to Coach Cal. Tyson was drinking from his five-gallon water jug which they all made fun of. And Felix. Where was Felix? Paul's strained eyes scanned the large gathering of athletes. Then he found him. He was standing close to the finish with his hands on his hips, talking privately to a man in beige slacks. Paul did not know the man. Paul turned toward the rest of the team, but his hunting eyes kept flickering back to Felix and the private conversation he was having with the mystery man in the beige pants and navy polo. He saw the two of them shake hands. As the man was walking away, Paul saw the emblem of a large which G on the breast of his polo. G for Georgetown, he thought. Paul was speechless. His heart sped. A stone sat in his throat.

Paul! There you are, Coach Cal called, which brought him back. The happy coach came striding over and shook Paul's limp hand. He shook his head.

Momo and I were just talking about how well you and Felix ran.

Uh huh, Paul replied, glazed and without a lick of emotion.

Yeah, we were saying he almost caught you there at the end. But you held on well and finished strong. Hey, you've got something on your lip, Paul.

Paul moved his hand across his mouth and cleared a chunk of white mush.

You feeling ok, Paul? Coach Cal said. He noticed Paul small trembles and how he seemed to be holding his ankle off the ground gingerly.

Paul looked down at himself as if he was noticing for the first time. He had a momentary spike of pleasure, glad to divert Coach Cal's attention from the race to something else. He rubbed the outside of his eyes and lifted his foot off the ground, giving it a weak shake.

He caught his lower lip in his teeth, said, You know, it does feel funny. I don't know if I tweaked it coming around that last bend, or actually, you know, that sidewalk up there by the restrooms just sort of drops off into the grass. I sort of rolled it as I was coming down. I guess whoever was paving didn't fill it in right, but I guess either way I should give it some rest and elevation. It does feel funny.

We've got plenty of ice over there, Coach said. Go on and rest up. Great run again.

It was Paul's shifty way of getting out of Coach Cal's overbright presence and resuming his own machinations.

Paul sat down on the lid of the team water cooler and watched Felix as he came back, not saying much, but shaking a few hands, and all around looking to Paul like some meek and pat newspaper delivery boy. Not a champion, not a form runner, but some hippie faced kid with no commitment, no drive, no time and no place on the scorecard as far as Paul was concerned.

Felix saw Paul and congratulated Paul on another good run. He stuck his hand out. Good race, he said.

Instead of taking his hand to shake, Paul covered his (not bum) bum ankle, a diversion. Yeah, thanks. How'd you do out there? Paul replied, as if he did not know.

Pretty well, Felix said. You edged me out at the end.

When he saw that was the extent of Paul's interest in the conversation, he walked away. At his back, Paul could hear the other boys congratulating him. Paul remained on the water jug, wringing his hands and looking past the tents of competitors to the barren course. His hand went to his false ankle, stroking it, as if he were calculating something in his mind. If ever a miserable runner lived, a soul who found no satisfaction from a victory despite it being close at the end, it was Paul seated on the water jug, Paul stroking his ankle, Paul with his eyes resting on nothing and his mind replaying that brief interaction between Felix and the coach with the Hoya logo on his shirt.

Paul stood to call the team together. But his thoughts were so scattered and the noise in his head so loud, he did not hear the team migrate from the pile of bags to the back of the bus, to watch another one of Felix's spontaneous dance performances. Paul could not bear it. Senseless with anger, he unscrewed the white lid to the water jug and dumped half out on the ground, so that it was light enough to carry. Then he hoisted it up to his chest and without warning carried it toward his team, whose backs were turned and who were very much absorbed. Another thick, racing hip hop beat rattled the air.

Felix flipped on the ground to perform some b-boy move, but as he began, Paul broke through the group and dumped a heavy slush of ice water on him. Not just the water and the ice, but the lid and jug came crashing on his head, flattening him to the ground in a shivering sop. Sam, Dave and Tyson cheered, thinking it was a form of applause. Paul wasted no time putting on his act. He came to Felix and helped him up and gave him a few hearty smacks on the back.

It took Felix a minute to come to his senses. Paul raised his voice over the boombox, which got toppled with the dump and was pulsing into the ground.

There you go, Felix, there you go, man. We all wanted to make sure we noticed the great run you had today, coming in close with a strong finish and helping the team get another win under our belts. You really showed a strong effort, and it came through and it really showed.

He said a few more things, all to the same effect. Every word was cheap. Every word was hollow. Every word sounded like it was cut off the back of a Wheaties box. Felix did not know this. He felt maybe this was one of the ways Paul showed approval, showed he accepted you, that the team accepted you.

So he sat there shivering on a pile of muddy ice, with a thin smile on his face, damping the cold wet hair which laid flat on his head like a painted on helmet. While Paul was beaming on his soap box, Momo tossed the freezing kid a towel and said to Paul, Is this your way of making him an official part of the team, since he didn't get to do primal scream?

The thought had never crossed Paul's mind. But he saw it as an opportunity to cover his real motive, which was a praise-haze. Paul made a bashful shrug, like he had been caught in an act of sportsmanship and sincerity. Paul wanted to ride his warm wave of admiration. Paul glanced around and saw Tits standing apart from the group, pulling bags together on the ground.

Paul said, Tits, what you doing all the way over there?

Picking up our bags, he said.

I can see that, can't you see we're having a team moment?

Tits lifted his eyes just enough to show he saw through every bit of pandering going on. The look pierced Paul's pride.

Paul said to him again, louder, Why don't you get over here and pretend you're on the team.

I don't need to pretend. I am on the team.

Well then, get over here and join our team meeting.

Tits dropped the bag in his hand. Is that what you call it?

Yes it is. But if you want to stand off by yourself like an island of bad thoughts, be my guest.

Tits face, the face famous for its perpetual shine and smile, mirrored back an expression he couldn't read. A knowing look. A look that began to gnaw away at Paul's cowboy smirk.

Paul put his hands out wide, and with a motion that encompassed the rest of the team, said, You know Tits, you're free to do whatever you want. If you want to stand over there and throw your bad vibes, no one's going to stop you.

But Tits was quiet. He packed the bags. He was quiet with knowledge, and the knowledge made him confident, and the confidence made him quiet. He knew something none of the others knew. A piece of knowledge wavering in his thoughts like a piano on the ledge of a balcony. And when the knowledge came there would be a crash, a smashup of iron strings and splintered wood, splattered keys and dead music.

Bottle the fire

Whatever happened to the romance of running; that primitive lovefeast between body and earth, between time and intensity; that symphonic high that could lift a body out of itself, could transfigure a dreary landscape into some jacob's ladder reaching up to that sweet throb of living?

By the end of their last meet, the team looked wilted, weak, and weathered. They went through all the motions of team life, and yet it was not team life. Paul continued presuming himself to be the mouthpiece of Press. But at best he copied Bill's bark only, used it to file guys down, to fan their hostility toward Felix and Tits and anyone else that crossed him.

But he was missing something.

Speed was a thing of beauty to Press. It's what turned him on and made his mind electrify with excitement. He spoke of it the way the poets wrote about love and sailors spoke of the sea, being their mistress and their maiden; their bondage and their liberty. Was running difficult? Yes. Demanding? Yes. But it was also full of aching desire, as sensual as a woman, and as mysterious.

It was not brute speed, or mechanical speed that turned Press on - it was what he liked to call *naked* speed. The difference between brute speed and naked speed was the difference between a bullet and an arrow. A bullet leaves with a bang and reaches its target with shattering finality. There was only one path for a bullet to take. But an arrow dances, quivers, swims through the air. It does not shoot. It flies.

Over his long career Press admitted he had only known two runners who he considered naked runners, arrows. But he would not say who they were. He knew the power of suggestion. He knew for the vast majority of his runners, it would do them no good to know where they stacked up on his list. Moreover, he did not build a team around arrows. Arrows were like Lamborghinis. When you saw them you admired them for what they were. Many of the kids he coached were bullets, and many more of them pellets.

But whether a kid was an arrow, a bullet, or a pellet, he wanted all of them to *bottle the fire*. That's one phrase he used that Paul neglected. Bottle the fire…by which he meant: hold onto that once in a lifetime feeling of moving free and unfettered over the ground. That matchless sensation of well-trained limbs synchronized and smooth. Bottle the fire of being 18 years old, green and verdant, with all your roads before you, with your hormones in high drive, and a strong beating heart and a mean kick and a body lithe and limber, and disciplined enough that you could get off the runway and ascend past the weary clouds of mediocrity at will. Realize that now, not last year and not five years from now, when you're through college and wondering what you'll make of yourself - but now, when your hard ass coach berates you for running like a pansy and not like the runner you're capable of running like, is a feeling you'll want to hold onto, recapture. The feeling that provoked you after practice, to tear off your shirt in a rash of rebellion, throw your bag down and walk cocksure, with the wide swinging arms, back to the track, back to the line. Even though your legs are dead with lactic buildup and your teammates tell you to get back here, and what the hell are you doing? And you tighten your laces once more and you find your mark and ditch your watch, that stupid calculating menace, behind you. And now your team has followed you around the fence of the bleachers just to see what kind of dickwad move you're trying to prove against your hard ass coach who's already left. It's you and your ego and the empty lane and the scorching track where heat wobbles off the surface. And you can hear them egging you on, saying *balls to the wall, grinders find a way, run or be dust.* You silence them by asking one of them to count you down. Like magic, your lungs, which gave out on you not fifteen minutes ago, fill again. Your heel bounces. Your eyes sharpen. Thighs twitch. Even the gnarly blister hanging off your little piggy and rubbing against the inside of your shoe begins to feel part of that agonal ecstasy coach said was reserved for a runner who was no longer content to chase the glory of a good time, or first place in a pageant. But was eager to outdo itself, to find its true limits, to drive a nail through past letdowns, and backhand the old man Resistance, who was always smooth talking, telling you you gave it your best go, the little liar in the back of your head, flattering you with 'that's enough, don't push it'…

You bring all this to the line.

If you were wise enough to bottle that feeling the second before 'Go', of absolute weakness and absolute confidence and absolute madness, and hold onto it, to break over your later years like a perfume, a scent leading you back to freedom, back to lost fervor and the pulse of life, than you should. Not to was unforgivable. That's what Press meant.

And that's what Paul was missing.

Dr. Hughes

The others remembered the saying, and the others, without Paul's insistence, reminisced about Press in their own way. They missed his tenacity and his hard-boiled outlook. Sometimes other teachers chided him for lacking sensitivity and perspective. For being 'one dimensional'. For "accidentally" passing around his answer key with the test so he had nothing to grade, in the remedial algebra class he taught.

'Is that the kind of man we want coaching these kids?' they'd say. 'Making them feel like all their life is cross country?'

If Press caught wind of his detractors, he either got so red with anger you could boil beans on his forehead, or he put ear defenders on and wouldn't listen to another word.

One sleepy afternoon in AP US History, Dr. Hughes, an ex-Princeton professor turned beloved high school teacher, opened fire on him. He had finished the day's lesson and decided to go off on Press.

He spoke in a calm, reasonable voice. The class was quiet. People did not take aim at Press lightly or often, despite their disagreements about his style. But Hughes had the stature to. And for whatever reason he did that day, and the class fell to a hush and the lesson they were going over disappeared to the background.

He said, Some coaches at this school, who will not be named, think they get the best out of their team by running their students into the ground, verbally abusing them, and calling it empowerment and motivation. Call it what you will, but it sounds a lot to me like the slavery we've been studying…

There were two runners in that class. One of them was Paul, and the other was Tyson. Their other classmates thought one of them would speak up, either agreeing with Hughes or defending Press. After Hughes made his point, the class turned to Paul and he sort of sidestepped the matter by saying, That's one perspective. You get used to the hard training though.

That only gave Hughes another moment to strengthen his point, which he did by bringing the class around to their earlier discussion of slavery in the south. He said, transitioning smoothly, The case for slavery, one of the reasons it persisted, is because there was a culture that preserved it. From within and without. Slave owners were dependent on it. But slaves too became desensitized to their condition, even insufferable conditions.

It took no big brain to see the line he was drawing between slavery and Press. And it appeared all the more poignant because the only other runner in the class was Tyson. Tyson Ray. The team called him Rayman. Not because of his name only, but because he resembled a stingray. Mellow in personality, he had wide shoulders that tapered to a skinny waist and a long, smooth stride when he ran. He was the one black cross country kid in the last ten years.

Now his classmates turned to him. Summoned to stand on one side or the other, he cleared his voice and said with surprising eloquence, something that stayed with Dr. Hughes and his classmates for a long time after.

He said, I get your point. Press is a hardass for sure. Some days I hate his guts. But the difference between the slavery of old and the slavery you suggest is that all of us on the team choose to be there. Those slaves weren't choosing to be there. And one more thing: cross country ain't everything, but it's a lot like everything. You got egos and clowns. You got winners and wimps. Good races and bad. You've got valleys and hills, straightaways, and the clock's ticking. And when you're in the race there's no time for pissing, you gotta race. If you catch what I mean, Dr. Hughes…

Tyson

He fairly well summarized the narrow mind of Bill Press. And he fairly well summarized for himself why he continued to run, despite the conditions, and despite other resistance too. He and his brother were raised by their grandmother. His grandmother was a steelcut woman with a large bottom. She made it clear to him she did not like running, and did not understand why her talented grandson ran. Running was for poor people, she said. She often disparaged him and compared him to his twin brother who played on the football team and had recruiters interested in him.

I don't understand why you run and only run. Why don't you put your athleticism to good use. I don't see the use of you going round in circles fast for as long as you do. That sounds boring as hell to me. Why don't you try something else. Get yourself a scholarship playing football, catching touchdowns. You'd be playing at homecoming if you did. No girls are coming to a homecoming foot race. I'm sure not. But if you'd play football, I'd come. Put those legs to use, you're wasting them the way I see it.

He got that week in, week out. Some weeks it was hard to defend. Hard to explain to her and to himself why instead of catching touchdowns, he stepped into harness and ran circles for a sad scold of a man. His freshman and sophomore year he preserved his pride by telling himself and his teammates (when Press wasn't around) that football was his real sport and running was his hustle. That once junior year came around he was going to switch. But then junior year came and he didn't. At times it brought him to a point of utter frustration and disappointment. He felt brainwashed, like he had missed his chance. He would call up in his mind a full, fragrant image of Bill Press to hate and throw knives at. He could see the man shaped like a capital D; not rough around the edges, but rough everywhere. He could see the greasy, one-shower-a-week hair and smell the day's old tequila. The car ashtray full of cigar stubs and the passenger seat piled with a dozen potato salad containers. This is what he chose. This is who he ran for.

But then he ran. Or he was run. Miles and miles with legs and lungs on fire. 8 days out of 10 it was hell, or close to it. But one day would come, or two, when there was no sucking wind, no breathing through sawdust. One day when the running flowed as smooth and clear as springwater. One day when a mental ceiling shattered, and running was not hell, but an outrageous happy hell. Wine and meat for the spirit.

Tyson lived in a house with a long driveway. Some days in the summers he was so burdened by his grandmother's disapproval he would go outside where the driveway stretched long ahead of him, a quarter mile with green grass on either side.

He would stare at it a long time, collecting his thoughts, letting his anger boil over. The driveway moved him. The longer he stared at it the more it seemed to undulate and shimmer like something alive. Whether it was a trick of his eye, or the heat in the air, the sight of it replenished some hunger in him for straightness and discipline and excellence. It was an ugly straightforward thing. It reminded him of Press. It disappeared to the edge of the road, which seemed to be the edge of the world.

It was rough and straight. Humped and straight. Crooked in places, broken in places, crowded by weeds and swamped by mud in places, and still desperately straight to the end.

It was a runway. A javelin aimed at the heart of the sky. Its straightness pulled his eye and all the landscape toward it like a magnet. And into that everblazing straightness, he began to run. Running drove out anger, routed bitterness, untied a thousand tangles in the heart. If he thought of Press, he would think how he hated his face and how he missed him. And that thought too would pass.

Mortal reserves

Press would recreate the workout of famed runners like Emil Zatopek, who during the lead up to the 1952 Olympics ran 400m intervals for ten consecutive days. He wanted them to tap his runner's 'vital reserves', a term coined by the American psychologist, William James. Vital reserves were latent abilities most men never realized because they hid below the surface of ordinary exertion. They were never tested, never called forth. Press wanted his runners to touch and feel and taste the deep running currents of untapped stamina and speed, the seldom used jolts he knew were there.

Vital reserves, he'd say, You've all got 'em. Some with more and some with less. It's just a matter of *will* you use them or not. If you're on this team, you've got no choice. You're the resource and I'm the drill. You're the stubborn ground and I'm the augur.

But if it was true there was something like vital reserves lying untapped below the surface of a man's living, then it was equally plausible there was the other side, too, mortal reserves, that once tapped began to flow with equal intensity - a negative potential, a river of decay polluting all it comes in contact with. But like all vital reserves, like all streams and rivulets, it had a small and almost trivial starting point and only became strong as it carried downstream, with gravity's help.

So, something similar began to happen to Paul. A trickle of something darker and more menacing than his usual meanness. One sign of it was the way he tossed the water jug on Felix and masked it over with his smile. But there were other details too, other mannerisms that spoke of something deathly and unwell.

On the bus ride back, he decided not to talk to Dave or Sam, but instead told them he was going to catch up on some homework, which was totally out of character. He held himself against one of the windows and removed a folder from his bag with assignments in it, and pretended he was doing something responsible with it. Sam and Dave left him alone for a while, and when they looked back to see how he was coming along, they saw on his face a look that was hard to place. It was both focused on what it was working on, but also wicked, though not overtly - and it was something they felt more than they could identify with words.

Dave whacked Paul's backpack which he had set up like a barrier between him and them. Paul flinched, snapped to attention. He said, Yeah, I'm doing good, just working on some funny things.

Funny things?

Paul made a dismissive wave. It's nothing really, he said, and closed his notebook until they left him alone again. Then he took it out again and continued working on something. They could see his mouth forming silent words.

A few minutes later, as they were talking, Paul punched the seat in front of him, a hard, vicious punch. But when they asked him if everything was ok, he had only a bland, confused expression on his face and he said, What do you mean?

Dave said, Why'd you punch the seat?

Paul looked at the seat with the indentation of his fist in it as if it were news to him what he'd done. A glazed look washed over his eyes. He said, Dave, you know what I was thinking?

What's that?

How far have you gotten with Casey yet?

Casey was Dave's longtime girlfriend. The strange, unrelated comment caught Dave off guard. He made no reply, unsure how to read Paul.

Well, what about it, Davey? Didn't you say she only ever wanted to got to -

Paul! Sam jumped in. You alright man?

What do you mean Sammy? I'm good, all good, he said, rolling his glazed eyes back out the window.

You been drinking enough water, Paul? Are you dehydrated?

Oh Sammy, sammy, sammy. You're too good to me. You're too good to everybody on this team. You're the angel of this team.

Now that he was talking more, and talking freely, they could tell something was definitely the matter.

He said, I'll tell you boys straight. I'm not trying to pull anything funny on you, and I can see you're looking at me like I've lost my head, but here's the secret. It's not me, it's coach.

Sam and Dave were glancing from the back of the bus to the front, trying to see if others had caught on to this unusual behavior. They had not. They scooched in closer, all their attention locked on him.

Yeah, yeah, yeah, come in closer boys, let's get our powwow on like the good ol days. Like I was saying, it's not me its coach.

Coachy…

He slipped his hand behind his bag and flashed a nip of whiskey.

It took them a second to register they were seeing what they were seeing, but when they did, they smiled in relief.

He rattled the nip again. They both declined. He said, Alright, suit yourselves, but later we're going out to celebrate. He put the bottle back in its hiding place and tore a page out of the spiral notebook he had in his lap and threw it up to the front of the bus where the others sat. It hit Kirby on the back of the leg and he picked it up and unfolded it. It was a page with the name Tits written on it about a hundred times and each of the names was scratched out with thick dark lines. Like some kind of sick joke an eight year old makes.

Paul caught Kirby's glance and whirled his finger for him to turn the page over. On the back Kirby found an unsavory illustration of the namesake. Kirby frowned, crumpled the junk and stuffed it in his pocket. He ignored Paul from thereon. Paul tore two more sheets out and threw them the same way and Kirby picked them off the floor and disposed of them immediately instead of dignifying them by opening.

Paul turned to his confreres. He whispered, I get it, I get it, you guys are giving me that look like what's going on with Paul. Why's he acting so weird? Well the truth is I've been thinking to myself I probably need to loosen up a little, right? It is our senior year and we all have sweet scholarships and are going off to good schools, and all we've done the past couple years is work, work, work, grind, grind, grind, and what's the harm if we cut loose a bit. Still run, still give it a fair go and turn on the jets when we need, but you know, cut some slack where slack's needed and not get all twisted up and knotted if you catch where I'm coming from.

As he whispered, the whiskey whispered off his breath. Sam and Dave drank it all in, this confession of Paul. He slipped his hand behind his bag to offer them the nip, but again they declined. Perhaps they were stupefied more than anything else. They did not know *this* Paul. They could not place him. He was everywhere, unspooled - the kid they knew better as the soldier of the track, the all American, the all AP classes honor student, contender for the senior superlative 'best all around'.

He went on unspooling, trashing Tits and trashing Cal, and boasting of his recent win. Twice he told Dave he should either dump Casey before the end of the year, before going off to college because it wouldn't last if he left and she stuck around and went to the state school - and if it was him (not that he was giving advice, just his opinion) he'd dump her in his head first, then push her to third and see if she'd go, and if not, tell her how he thought she loved him, and if she went, then good for him, and if not then dump her for real and don't look back because you'll have all the fish in the sea by the time you get to college. And he ended his miserable drunkwise sermon by losing his place in what he was saying and staring off into space, And then Felix, he mumbled…Felix…I forgot to say about Felix…

He drifted off. His head nodded toward the seat back in front of him, the one he threw a punch at twenty minutes prior. Half awake, he took his hand to rub his nose and smeared blood over his top lip. When Sam and Dave saw it, they snatched the bag away from his side and saw that he had been scraping his thigh with the rough edge of the nip cap, screwing it into his flesh over and over until it bled steadily down his leg.

He laughed and laughed and kicked them off him, saying, I can hold my own. I'm not a girl. He saw the mess he made and wiped his leg with his backpack, saying, It's only a fleshy-fleshy-flesh wound. The price you pay for being number one.

He nodded some more, slurred some more. He rubbed his lazy hand down his face again, marking himself red, said, Now, who was I talking about, who was I just talking about?

He put the bottle cap in his mouth and moved it around like a marble. Then he removed it and held it with two fingers and made stupid shapes with his saliva on the back of the seat to match the stupid, nonsensical things he was saying, or trying to say. And all the while his friends contained him in the back, worried what to do, how to respond.

He had one more thing to say, but as he searched for words that would not come, he fit the sharp cap between his lips and moved it slowly from one side of his mouth to the other, the exact same way Press would move his stub of cigar during summer training.

Paul was fading. Now, what was I saying, what was I…? His voice trailed off and his eyelids fluttered. As he nodded asleep he jerked away at the last moment and flinched. His hand tore in the air like someone was throwing a punch his way and he was trying to stop it. The empty blow caught him instead. In the flash of motion, the cap dislodged from his lips and scraped down the side of his face leaving a clean red slice from the top of his lip down the ridge of his jaw. The foolish cut spouted a trickle of blood. But he did not notice, did not feel it, did not care. His eyes closed and he konked out cold.

Paul, out

The name Felix was the last thing on Paul's mind when he went out cold.

Thankfully, his teammates were there to offer assistance. They were not far from the school at that point.

Sam and Dave called Kirby to the back of the bus because his dad was a firefighter and they knew he had some first aid training, beyond the basics. The two others cleared the space and Kirby sat down next to Paul, who was piled over like a bag of bones.

A few slaps on the face, a few name calls, a few shakes of his arm, a cold bottle of water on standby, and before long he was there.

He came awake suddenly, like a machine whose power had been unplugged. The eyes flipped, then the twisted neck came around and the slumped posture - all of it returned bolt upright, and a slow, heavy breath returned and began to quicken, and he stared at Kirby like an unblinking stone for twenty seconds or so before saying, What are you doing back here?

I was checking on you.

Kirby was trying to get one last look at Paul's eyes to see if they were dilated or not, but he got no chance because Paul pushed him off and told Sam and Dave not to let him back here again.

What was he doing in the first place, he said, like he had no memory of what was happening before he hit the wall…

Did you know you went to sleep or…Dave began in a timid way, careful not to say anything that might stir his anger.

The thick furrow driving through the middle of Paul's forehead darkened, though his eyes did not move.

Really, he said. What are you guys doing, or you're pulling something on me because I've got a killer headache and I've got a shit ton to do for my schooling, and I'm, I'm finished with my running for the day.

My schooling…my running. What were these odd phrases coming out of his mouth? Although he was conscious and awake, and strangely sober, there was something off about Paul. He had just run a tough race. He was severely dehydrated, as evidenced by the chapped lips and pale complexion. They gave him three full water bottles and he downed them fast as a dog on a summer day.

Sam held up his fingers and said, Can you tell me how many you see here? How many fingers I'm holding up.

Eight.

Now, how many? Sam put his hands behind his back like he was shuffling them around and then brought them out holding the same six up.

Uh… uh…Three, Paul said, sticking his front teeth out and making a dufus voice. Six, six, six, alright Sam. Now get your stupid fingers out of my face. Stop playing whatever game you're playing.

He chugged another water bottle. The bus came to a stop. The team up front was staring back at the situation with Paul, but Dave made a motion across his neck for them to turn around.

They said nothing, not any of them. Paul stood up and took his bag and said, Where are we again?

Sam told him plainly that they were back at the school. They had just come from Bull Run, but before he could say more, Paul punched him.

I already knew that, stupid, he smirked. Now, let's all break because I got to get back to my schooling…

There was that phrase again…and that was the end of that bizarre episode.

Team gathering

The following day Paul missed practice. He never missed practice. And the day after that he was late, and that was unlike him too because he was a stickler about start times and end times, and he always got a few extra brownie points with Press (not that he needed them) because he was the guy who proposed the whole team did hill intervals instead of a short run if someone came late.

No one said anything to him, no one made any comment about his timeliness or his whereabouts the day before. The other captains briefly mentioned something to Coach Cal about what happened on the bus, but he was not too concerned and even suggested it might be a good thing for him to rest up if his body was telling him to slow down and rest up. Especially before the final high stakes quarter of the season.

That allayed their worries some. After practice, when Paul left, the team got together and talked about how it seemed Paul had been especially hard on himself the past couple weeks.

It was a boiling day. No one was in any rush and they sat together on the grass beside the track, some with their backs on the ground and their legs propped up against the chain fence. They were half pulling weeds and half discussing what to make of Paul's condition and half watching the girls team go by on the track. Which they didn't mind.

Sam spoke up. I've known Paul for a long time and he's always kept a lot close to his chest. I haven't seen anything out of the ordinary the past couple weeks. Apart from the bus ride back. That worried me some. But aside that, nothing more than you'd expect for a kid like Paul, who's got all that on his plate.

The idea circulated for a moment. Then Momo flicked a weed off his fingers and replied, Yeah, I don't know about that...what about the showers he's been taking?

Showers? What do you mean? Dave said, You mean the cold showers he used to take super early on race days to psych himself up for a big race. He's been doing that since freshman year.

No, I'm not talking about the cold showers. The hot ones, like really hot.

That got their attention. He glanced around to see if anyone else knew what he was referring to.

Oh, you haven't seen this? I saw it once or twice last week because I had to stay late to finish up some extra credit stuff. On my way out I usually go through the gym because it's shorter than going all the way around the main hall. Usually there's no one in there because either all the teams are out practicing or done for the day. I go in there and it's steamed up to the windows. You know how it gets in winter when everybody's in there. It was like that. Anyway, I'm going along, minding my own because I'm not trying to be some Jarred Jeffries creeper - you guys remember that? Tits does. Right Tits? When Jeffries got busted snapping pics on his flip phone. That's another story. Like I was saying, I wasn't creeping, I was just making my way through, but I was kind of curious because I could still hear showers on, and when I passed by the lockers I glanced down the middle aisle real quick and saw him there, sort of hiding off to the side. With like three or four showers on. Just him. I could see his duffle sitting on the bench and his clothes and that showerhead freaking beating down on him. That thing was roasting, like the knob turned all the way to the left. And everybody who's ever taken a shower in there knows rule no. 1 is you never turn the knobs all the way left. Never. That's like basic knowledge. Nichols even wrote up that stupid warning memo at the beginning of the year, posted it all over the walls in the locker room, telling people not to turn the knobs too far because people had gotten burnt. They were supposed to get someone to fix it, but they never did, because I've tested it and it'll still peel your skin off. I saw him for two seconds or so. That knob cranked all the way over, and all I could think of was dam - or, as my people say, que fuerte…I'm going to the exit and I hear the shower stop and he calls out, Hey Momo. I stop. Give him one of those quick waves like I'm just passing through. And he goes, wassup? And I told him I had to stay for extra credit.

Yeah, your extra credit for your stupid Latin class, Tits laughed, pulling a weed and launching it at him.

Momo smiled. Yeah, it actually is a stupid Latin class. I only took it because my dad said it would help me with my English, and I'm like Dad, I'm fluent in English. I'm bilingual. But he's like no, you're taking Latin. So I'm taking Latin. Hating Latin. That's one thing, thanks for getting me off track, Tits. The other thing, the main thing I was saying was I told Paul goodbye and all he says is, *Alrighty then*. You know, like he doesn't say bye like a real person. He says, *Alrighty then,* kind of blows you off. And Press would say the very same thing all the time too. He said that to me a couple times the first year I joined the squad. And I thought what a jackass. Do I really want to run for this jackass, and look at me now. Apparently I do or I wouldn't be telling these stories.

Are you done talking? Sam said.

Yeah, I'm done…Wait!

Alright, good.

No, wait! One more thing. Last thing, promise. It's the thing I thought of first actually. I saw Paul a second time doing the same thing, but this time…

Alright! Now you're cut off for good, Dave pushed him over on the grass. You've officially proved that we have a new Jarred Jeffries on our hands, so beware boys. Keep your eyes peels for a peeping Mexican whose go-to locker room alibi is "extra credit Latin"

The team broke out laughter and they tossed sweaty shirts and plucked weeds at him.

Well I guess that's one thing to add to story along with the bus ride stuff. Sam shook his head. I think that was him horribly dehydrated, combined obviously with the alcohol, with him being fried from the race, and all the lead up. The kid doesn't sleep the night before races. But somehow he comes out and gets it done.

Shrugs all around. Thoughtful stares. More plucked weeds.

Is that two strikes then, Sam? Dave asked, speaking for the team. You've known him the longest and you know him the best. Would you call that two?

Sam bit his lip. I don't know. What happens at three?

We tell someone what's going on, Tyson joined.

We don't know what's going on. Sam said.

Yeah, that's the point, Tyson added.

All we know is that he's been acting a little off, Sam said.

Little?! Little!? Momo exclaimed. Well shit. I'm glad y'all aren't my friends. Because if I was going in burning myself in the shower I hope someone would do something, but that's just me. What about you guys? Tits, you jumpin in?

They turned to Tits. He sat on the ground with his legs clasped together with his hands. He had an even look on his face. Again, nowhere in sight was the big smile they were used to seeing from him. His eyes lowered. With all their attention on him, he almost looked like he was about to break down and cry. Momo sat beside him. He leaned toward him, to get him to talk.

You know anything, Tits?

I might, he said.

You might? Or you do?

I do. But I don't think it's the right place for it.

Hey man, you can't just drop something like that on us and not tell.

I'll tell, but not now. It wouldn't do any good. I wouldn't do Paul any good. I'll put it that way.

Shouldn't Sam know it at least?

Tits shook his head.

Well can you at least give us a clue…? Is it information?

Tits turned his face to the side, considering the question.

I wouldn't call it information, he said.

Is it a rumor?

No.

Is it knowledge?

Yes.

About Paul?

Yes.

TEAM GATHERING

Only Paul?
No.
Would this knowledge be bad if it got out?
Depends.
And how did you acquire this knowledge?
Tits paused, spat on the ground between his legs.
So, how did you…?
I stole it, Tits said.

Without even knowing what it was, jaws dropped. It was Tit's, the goodiest good boy on the team.

Tits!! Momo slapped him on the arm. You?? You stole something?

I wasn't intending to at first. But when I saw it, I knew what it was and I took it.

So it's a thing?
It's a thing.

Well howdie, howdie, howdie, Momo sang, taking the kid next to him by the forearm and rocked him side to side, trying to shake the knowledge off him…Is it me or is it getting hot in here? And did Tits Callahan just become the most interesting kid on this team?

The smiles went around. Tits tried to keep his expression level, but the more they looked at him the more he cracked some, then some more. The more he tried to lock it away, the more his old smile came out to play. It was only a matter of time.

Stalling

No matter what the knowledge was, it was good to be talking again. It was good to be shooting the breeze and laughing, ribbing and getting ribbed, opening up doors that were shut and all around venting the smothered feeling of resentment that had slowly choked their team spirit since the day Press quit.

It had been a long time. Longer than they realized. The resentment began at the retreat and developed through all the weeks hence. The team, despite its winning record, despite its pedigree, was tired. They felt some young, us against the world, vitality return. It was like coming in from a rainy run, a cold sopping run of all duty and no pleasure - and taking (no irony) a good, hot shower.

The conclusion of that meeting was: Sam would check on Paul, and Momo was undoubtedly a peeping Mexican, and Tits had a secret. And truthfully no one really cared about Tits' secret. What they cared about was that Tits smiled. The old happy face came out again.

Tits had the best smile on the team, a smile that as Kirby once aptly put it, reminded him of 'sunshine on the back of a cereal box.' They all knew what he meant. The smile was back, and that was good. Whatever Paul's situation was, whatever the mystery of his pain, what was important was that some balance was restored. Momo was talking and Tits was smiling. Dave still had a girlfriend and Sam, who felt like he had distanced himself from the younger guys to chaperone Paul, was back on good terms with them.

The ragtag conversation roused their spirits and raised their enthusiasm. Though there were two among them who were conspicuously quiet that afternoon. Felix and Kirby. Both joined in the chuckling, but neither offered their frank opinions. And there was good reason why.

They were preoccupied. As it happened, the two of them stayed behind when the group split up. They sort of lingered on the grass, got up, brushed themselves off, taking a long time to clean up their mess of clothes and shoes and water bottles and banana peels. Each was stalling in his own way, and each could feel the other stalling, but would not say.

Felix started drifting a few steps toward the parking lot. He looked back at Kirby. Kirby's hands were going through the motions of gathering things and putting on shoes, but all his attention was yanked off to the side, on the swinging pony tails and toned legs and pretty voices coming from the track.

You need a ride by chance, Kirb? Felix asked.

Kirby blushed, hesitated. He got up. His head hung in a look of defeat, and he turned to accept the offer, but then he froze and pivoted on his heel. He said, Actually I might, uh…I'm thinking about…

His jumbled reply made him blush more, made him more conscious of what he was doing, the big red giant, stuck between the track and the parking lot.

The girls team came round with their peals of pretty laughter rising and falling as they ran away. Kirby and Felix turned their heads in unison and they looked back and met each other in the eye and smiled the same goofy smile.

What are you doing? Kirby said to Felix.

No, you tell me what you're doing, Felix came back at him.

They were playing conversational footsie. Neither one wanted to be the first that made the move, or admit what he was doing. But it was obvious. In that sweet window, as they looked on, they had no thought of stroke volume, or finishing times, or fast twitch muscles, or any of the frivolous running nonsense that filled their heads. They were just two stalling kids. Two guys looking for girls. Two guys tongue tied.

I'm the one that asked you if you wanted a ride and you stalled, Felix said.

Well, yeah, but if you really were just interested in giving me a ride you'd have turned right around there and taken your own self home, but you tiptoed on back here.

Kirby laughed at the situation.

You think there's anything as pretty as a girl that runs fast? he said.

I think they're pretty standing still too, Felix replied.

Yeah, touche…just tell me we're not both here for the same girl.

His laugh caught the girl's attention as they were finishing their cool down. The bashful redness returned to his face and he quickly turned his back. He shook his head and covered his smiling mouth with his big hand. He passed his hand over his big shaggy mane in a messy way to divert the noise he made.

His stomach churned. It felt like standing on the starting

line before a race. It felt like eagerness, like it's now or never, like she's just standing over there and what am I doing getting all red in the face and beating around the bush talking to *him*. The longer he stood thinking about it the more he felt it, and the more he kept messing up his hair and getting angry at himself for just standing there.

He was big and red and restless. His doubts gnawed at him. The longer he waited to do something the more he felt he would never do it, that he would chicken out and just go with a group of guys again, even though he was sick of going to dances with guys. He had been going to dances with guys and running with guys and talking to guys all his life. But now he wanted a girl, a date to take to the dance. And maybe just maybe, taste a bit of that high school dream.

The stalling felt like an eternity. It was already late. It was past the time he told himself he was going to do it, the time he planned in his mind, after he saw her in class that afternoon and they talked for a few minutes about their seasons. The doubts lumped in his throat. He grew redder and redder, and his nerves turned to anger. He was not an angry guy, but now he was angry at Felix for getting in his way and slowing him up and being a good for nothing, cock blocking…

Suddenly he heard a click. His racing thoughts riveted. It was the sound of the gate opening. When he turned, he saw Felix striding toward the ladies on the far side of the track.

His anger turned to panic. *What was he doing? What was he doing? That no good son of a gun, with balls on him though, going right up to them. And here I am standing like a fool, like a big clumsy no courage wallflower fool.*

He scuffed the ground, felt his clumsy hands at his side. Restless for something to do with them, he dropped to his knee and swept his hand through a patch of sticky weeds they had been plucking earlier. Unthinking he plucked one, stripped the sticky petals of the stem, leaving some on his fingers. He threw it down, disgusted with himself, and once again raked his weedy hands through his messy hair.

By sheer will power he drifted to the gate. The door was outswung like a hand inviting him forward. But he was afraid, now more than before, when he had planned on doing it solo. He leaned into the fence. He could feel his hot red ears ticking and feel the plastic smile on his face for all to see, and he hated it; he hated how he looked, and how big he was, and the sticky weed petals in his hair, and what was happening. Even though he had no idea what was happening.

He fidgeted and watched as Felix went right up to them. He watched how the girls turned and gave him their full attention. The ticking in Kirby's ears worsened, his swallowing lost all naturalness. If he could be a bird overhead and see himself from above, he'd see every physical feature on him jumbled and discombobulated like Mr. Potato Head. He could not hear the exchange. All he could see from afar was hand gestures, smiles. A guy talking to girls. And that guy was not him.

Just walk away Kirb, you lost, you lost. Just go back. You already look like an idiot, waiting for your stupid guy friend again so he can go and get the girl and make the move and you can't.

So disappointed. So furious with himself, he ripped his hands off the fence and left. But as he was going he heard his name. And it was not Felix calling his name.

It was her, Kara Klein. Coming his way. Her curly brown hair bounced at her shoulders and she was slinging her backpack, trying to catch up to him.

Hey Kirby, wait up! Felix said you wanted to see me. He was waving you over, but I don't think you saw. He came over and introduced himself, he's real nice. He's the fast one you were talking about, right? I can see it. He's got that runner look. But not the snotty one some of your guys have. I won't name names, she smiled.

Kirby caught about a half of what she was saying, because he was so delighted by her voice and so surprised that it was her talking to him. That was Kara. She was pretty and fun and could talk to a wall.

She was smiling at him, waiting for him to reply.

What was it, anyway Kirby? You wanted to talk to me? She threw him a humorous suspicious look. Like she would not budge unless he told her what he was planning to tell her.

All the words mushed out of his mouth. But they came out. He asked her to homecoming. All the fear he had felt creeping down his spine just moments before, was replaced by a calm he had no word for. And that was before she answered.

She said, I'd love to go with you. But I have one requirement. She thought about it. She placed her finger in the air, No wait, two! Two musts. One, you must keep me well hydrated and well fed, because this girl likes to dance, and this girl likes to eat. And you can't dance well if you haven't eaten well. But nothing fancy. I don't need salmon or steak or almond butter, if you know what I mean. Speaking of butter, I do love nutter butters. Nutter butters are good. Cosmic brownies? Not so much. They're a little bit trashy. Well, no, not trashy. I take that back. That's the wrong word. They're just not for me. So no cosmic brownies, ok? But nutter butters are in. What else? She stuck her foot out and tapped the ground. Then she smiled again, came up to him and gave him a hug. She backed up and lifted her head to look him in the eyes because she was about two feet shorter than he was.

So what's your second? he asked.

My second? Oh yeah!

The thought of what it was made her pull her arm across her face like she was about to sneeze, and let out a flurry of snickers.

You're going to love this…Number two is, you're going to be wearing a pink sequin blazer, slacks, and alligator skin dress shoes. Alright? We'll look smashing. And you can't say no. Ha ha ha ha…

She gave him another hug, and off she skipped.

Kick the hive

Kirby was a kite on a blue sky. He was a bouncy toy. He held the world on a string. His head was up and he had styled his hair and his teammates could hear his deep bellowing chuckle from down the hall and across the lunchroom all day long.

Kirby Spence was a new man. Between periods he looked for Felix. They had split up after the rendezvous on the track yesterday afternoon, and Kirby didn't have a chance to say thank you, or to say anything really.

When he saw him at his locker he almost bulldozed him. He gave him a hearty shake on both his shoulders.

There you are! Felix, you sly dog! You going to tell me what that was all about yesterday?

Should I be telling you, or should you be telling me? Mr hair slicked back and big smile going?

Kirby reddened, but it was a confident red. He said, yeah, I know. I'm doing it different today for a change. I got back last night after, well, hold on, back up dude. How'd you know?

How'd I know what?

Kirby hit him playfully.

Don't give me that bull. How is it that I turn around and Kara Klein's coming right after me.

She's the one you wanted to ask out right?

Yeah, but how'd you even know I was planning on that?

First of all, all practice long you were lost in the clouds. I noticed you kept looking over at the track while you were cooling down, and Momo nudged me a couple times and we saw you in another world.

Man, was I that much of a dead giveaway?

Yep. And all the time we were sitting on the grass talking, you were real quiet and usually you have something to say.

Hey, you were quiet too if I recall.

I'll give you that.

And I doubt you were going over your dance routine in your head too. So, what were you doing there too, first of all asking if I needed a ride. I thought maybe you were trying to throw me off or something, but then when we were talking and I looked back and you were going over there, you threw me for a real loop.

Good.

Good?

Yeah, you need to be thrown for a loop. You're too sweet sometimes. Too much of a gentle giant when you ought to be the big angry giant too.

I guess you're right. But when you went up there I had this thought that you were going after the same girl that I was, and that you were going to get her. My mind started heading off with all kinds of nasty thoughts, full confession. I was like, who's this good for nothing kid who doesn't know anybody. That's when I turned to go and I heard my name called and I look back and there she is jogging over to me. So explain yourself.

What do you want me to explain?

How did you know she was the one I wanted to ask out? Because I haven't told anybody about that.

It was a total guess actually. A good guess, I guess. For one, I knew what you were over there trying to do. But I figured she was the one you were interested in because when they were cooling down, every time she did a lap, you dropped your head and turned to me and say something stupid. You did it like three times.

Damn. That easy?

Like I said, it was a good guess.

And what about you? You were over there for the same reason weren't you?

I was.

Yeah I figured. Real smooth of you. Kara came over to me and said you were over there introducing yourself, to the girls team. At first I thought that's nice, but afterwards I thought there's no way he went over there just to introduce himself like that. No way. Who would do that? I mean you're an oddball, but you're not that much of an oddball.

I'll take that as a compliment, Kirb.

It is a compliment. That takes some boldness.

Bold or not, you had better luck than I did.

Kirby snapped his fingers all over the air.

Wait, you actually asked someone out? In front of all of them.

Sort of, Felix said lowering his voice to make sure no one passing by could hear.

Who, who?!

Bring it down a notch, big man. I'm not trying to tell the whole school.

All right, all right, but can you at least tell me what she

looked like, what was she wearing?

Did you see that girl in blue shorts?

Oh man. You mean the real fast one? The one out in front a lot.

Yeah, I think that was her. I think her name is Erin.

Kirby doubled over and had another good laugh. He tried to keep from making too much of a commotion in the hall.

What? Felix asked, Do you know her?

Yeah I know her. And just about everybody at this school knows her. Erin Spankson. They call her spanx.

Spanx?

Yeah, spanx. And here's the scoop. She's pretty, she's fast, and sadly she's also taken. She goes out with one of the guys on the baseball team and they've been together for a long time. That's all I know. So what happened? Was it smooth or awkward?

It was a little awkward. I think I must have said about three or four times that I wanted to come over and introduce myself, and they began to look at me like why is this kid still standing here. First time I said it I was actually pretty nervous and I went around and actually shook their hands. Which didn't help the awkward level. It's pretty intimidating when they're all standing together and… now what are you laughing about?

I'm sorry. I can't get over the fact that you just went up to them and started talking. And you shook their hands. And then you tried to ask out Erin Spankson.

Felix shrugged. He said I didn't think about it too much, I just went for it. At the end of the day though you're still the one who got the date and I'm the one running out of options.

Nope, you're not short of options. Any guy who's willing

to go up to a group of pretty girls he doesn't know and ask one of them out isn't going to be short of options. He might not get the first pick he was going for, but he won't be short of options I'll tell you that much. And I bet, and it's just my educated guess, you'll find someone even better. That's my bet.

Kirby hit him on the shoulder and turned the other way to head to class. As he was walking away he had a thought, and he spun back. He said, You know what, Felix, you're a mystery in your own right. Aren't you? We've all been so wrapped up with Paul, and meanwhile you hop right on to our team and in like three meets and a handful of practices you're already nipping at Paul's heels and chasing him down the runway and no one seems to have any common sense to say, what the hell?! And it's not like you're out there waving a flag or talking about your time. But seriously, what the hell?! I think we've all been afraid, to tell you the truth. We've all been afraid of someone breaking the status quo, of someone coming in, running like a fire bolt. Someone who has no connection to Bill Press. And we've all been sort of holding out, and holding back, like we're victims of some tragic loss, like we're all a bunch of lost sheep without Press here. It's beginning to clip for me. I can see it. We're stalling. We're like me standing at the gate wanting to go through and talk to the girl, but unwilling and too scared. Too afraid to shake it up.

The big giant was talking excitedly, in a fever of conviction. The class bell rang and it was just him and Felix in the hallway. The big guy tossed his hand above as if he didn't care that they were late. This was too important, what they were talking about, what had gone too long unspoken.

I think the other guys feel the same way to be honest, he said. Even Sam and Dave. They want more. You can feel it. They want more than padding their senior year with a couple nothing special runs and second places and then rationalize it all by talking to each other about the colleges they're going to. The new teams are going to be running for. Everybody's checking out, trying to contain the Paul show, trying to keep him from going off the rails. But I think that's already a done deal. I wish it wasn't, but I think it is.

Kirby's big passion echoed down the hall. And Felix, mysterious Felix stood there all while listening, feeling the passion growing inside him too. Kirby paused, then collecting his thoughts, seemed to recall the point that made him turn in the first place.

He took a wide stance and palmed his hands together, and the more impassioned he became the more he needed his palms together

What I wanted to tell you is, it's time we lit you like a fuse. Time to light the candle under your ass.

He glanced up at the hall clock, tossed his hand at it. He said, forget about that a second. It's time to put the wings on your feet and turn up the volume like the music you dance to on your boombox. Dude, you can tear Paul to shreds, pants him all the way down, give him a whipping. But you've been careful. You know what's going on. You're not dumb. But you don't want to step in too much and knock the hive over.

He put his finger on Felix's chest and pushed him backward. I've seen you run. I see what you can do. Kick it. Kick the damn hive over. Kick it. Kick the whole thing to shits and giggles. Stick it up Paul's…(as he was about to shout the word, a teacher passed on one side and Kirby sucked the word up

138

and said it with his eyes instead). Are you picking up what I'm putting down? Drop the hammer, Felix. Put your antlers on and buck. What's that word Momo was using the other day? That Latin word for More?

He knit his eyebrows and snapped his fingers trying to think of the word.

Magis? Felix said.

Magis! That's it! There, that's your word. You got it? That's your word from here on.

He put his hand out the shake and Felix took it.

With a nod the fiery pep talk ended and the two went their separate ways.

Dover Sands

Homecoming was fast approaching. A week and a half from Wednesday it would be there. Already the school was being dressed in red and white streamers. Already were car windows being painted and pregame plans and post game plans being made. Already were teams showing extra spirit with gift bags exchanged from bigs and littles. The principal, instead of his minute of wisdom on the intercom in the mornings, started playing a few seconds of band music to rouse the students and get them in the spirit.

On Wednesday the team had a light practice. Paul was there in Paul fashion, sniping at Tits for no reason, and asking Momo if his leg was finally healed or if it was going to be there for the rest of the season. He made his rounds. And finally he turned to Felix and asked if he had a date for the dance.

Felix said, Not yet.

Paul flipped his wrist like he was checking a watch. Better get moving. All the good ones are gone.

Kirby jumped in and said, Don't worry. He'll have a date by then. The good ones might be gone but the best ones no one even attempts. And they're ripe for the asking.

Paul was caught off guard by Kirby's boldness. In all the

years they ran together Kirby had not so much a said word to openly contradict Paul.

What's that Kirby? Paul said, Are you speaking up for the new guy? Giving him some sweet sauce to lift his spirits. That's kind of you. Or are you giving out your own advice? Will you be coming with Tits and Momo like usual, and drinking punch and dancing with other dudes?

The old Kirby would have dropped his head and absorbed the mean comment with a few soft chuckles. But the new Kirby, the revived Kirby, looked him straight on with a flinty expression. He brewed with quiet thunder.

Then he asked Paul an unthinkable question.

So do you have a date Paul?

Paul laughed, took a step back and knelt to tie his shoes. When he was down, he said to all the team, That right there is Kirby Spence gentleman. Son of Carl Spence, of the famous volunteer fire station and Spence Sanitary Solutions, in a nutshell. Can't even take a punch like a man and answer a question like a man. Has to spin it off, don't you? All right, he looked at Dave and Sam. What are we running today?

You never asked me a question, Kirby replied.

In fact I did.

You did not. You made some stupid remarks about me dancing with dudes, but you never asked me a question. I asked you, and you're the one that dodged.

Kirby, why don't you quit school early and start selling porta potties like your dad. All right? Are we running or are we running?

The spat ended there. It ended like all of them ended, with Paul having the last word, and having the last mean word. Being around Paul those days was like stepping around broken glass. There was only one thing to do with broken glass.

You swept it up.

At the meet the next day, the guns went off and the usual runners fell into their usual positions. Paul led the race from the beginning and Dave and Sam were his right and left guard. They were close behind him for the first stretch, tangling with a few runners from competing schools, but not many. They ran out of a course called Dover Sands, which was once a luxury golf course converted into a public park and trail network.

It was a course Bill Press liked to call the Fair Lady of the season. The hills were mellow, soft and sweet. Sand traps from the earlier golf course were repurposed into hazy pastures of waving heath grass. The grass itself retained its golden, grain like hue and the homes surrounding the area were large estates, multi-acre lots with pretty barns and well kept yards and infinity pools.

All the scenery made for a pretty run.

Because of its location and scenery, it made the race one of the most well attended among local fans, who could, if they wanted to, sit on white Adirondack chairs by the starting line in front of the old clubhouse, now wedding rehearsal venue and take it all in.

As tradition had it, the boys called the race My Fair Panties, a nod to Presses my fair lady, and a nod to a tradition they had every year of pantsing the winner of that meet after the race. That same pantsed victor was then required to give a pep talk, a press talk, beside the clubhouse. Most years since Paul had won, the pep talk and the picture of the postpantsed winner went into the school paper.

The day was fine. The hills were breezy and buxom. A cold blue sky ran high above the waves and lady curves of the brown-gold and fawn-colored course. From the start line, the trail was wide and straight and clean and gradually broke into dunes and shocks of tall grass. Something about that race reminded the boys of their best days on the beaches of rural Maine. The wind was a steady chant and the soft hills as they rose and fell were like the sway of the sea. Tall grass was like dune grass, and the gold stubble glistened in the noonday heat like boulders in the sun.

It was a fair race to begin, but as it got underway it got dirty. Two fast freshman twins, named Ryan and Cole Dupree, gained on the leader. They had a dirty tactic where one would run ahead of the other, and bounce between them the guy they wanted to overtake. The one in front, pushing the pace, would either block the path of the guy they were squeezing, or he would create a distraction with a loud yell or feign a fall, or something belligerent enough that it got in the head of Dave and Sam, but not enough that it broke any rules.

It was a tactic, a dirty tactic, but it worked. The first half of the race, Paul pulled well ahead and was coasting. But he heard the skirmish at his rear. As he reached the halfway mark, Ryan and Cole had snipped the gap and were close behind him.

All race day, aside from the Dupree twins, the race was like a pleasant jog in paradise. The main pack of runners, not the leaders, gelled together and stayed together as though they were all protecting the pleasantness among them.

There were gentlemanly passes, and gentlemanly right of

ways, and no flying elbows or labored breathing. From far off, as the little dots went up and over the swaths of dark yellow, it looked to be only a two horse race, and a question of whether the Duprees could ruffle Paul off his lead, or if Paul would spurn their threat as he did so many before.

Rather, something unlikely happened. A lone runner split the pack from behind. At first it looked like Kirby, but it was only Kirby making way. Felix Sun split the fair running flock. Some balked and some tried vainly to bring the pace up to his, but he was out of reach. Well out of reach.

It would be like seeing a sea of Camrys part and a Porsche, that had been lingering and hidden in its midst, press the pedal just slightly and wave them farewell in a wink.

Felix Sun winked. He winked past Dave, and he winked past Sam. He gobbled up the hard-nosed Duprees, ran right between them like he was toying with their game - and after a slight pause, a momentary hesitation when Kirby could see him calculating the cost of passing Paul, he routed the old hesitation, and flew.

He smoked him, dusted him, spanked him, and all very smoothly, and gentlemanly; as smooth as the lady hills and as sweet as the ladies who were gathered at the finish line to watch him clear the lead by twelve seconds.

In those long twelve seconds that marked the beginning of the end of Paul's reign, the Dupree twins took full advantage of the shocking pass which they could see took all the fight out of Paul. They caught up, pulled him into their mousetrap and set the spring. But they did not need to spring it because Paul sprung it himself. He pulled up two strides from the end holding his ankle, holding it in pain, and hobbling off the course through the finish in fourth place.

The stream of runners passed by. Meanwhile the All American, the golden boy, the chosen one, absconded timidly along the fringe of people, making no eye contact, but devoting all his attention to the tender care of his ankle.

No one cared. No one noticed. The crowd followed Felix, the pack rebel, the sunburst kid who they approached like some sort of exotic animal, congratulating him, but not knowing who they were congratulating. Most people had never seen him before.

Paul had not run poorly. The Duprees ran a hell of a race. All worthy of celebration. But Felix was worthy of awe.

Mild-mannered Coach Cal was the first to congratulate Paul on a good run and ask him about his ankle. Paul winced, said, It must be the same ankle that got me last time, when I was coming off the sidewalk, feels like the same place.

Coach Cal made him a bag of ice and sat down with him on the water cooler. He took a shoe off and inspected the area Paul was talking about. Coach Cal rolled the ankle softly, seeing if he could detect anything wrong with it, any swelling. He was talking to Paul, but Paul was not hearing well because he kept overhearing his teammates and other coaches congratulating Felix somewhere behind him.

Paul? Paul? Hey! It took a few calls to get his attention back. Paul turned.

Did you feel anything while I was moving it?

I couldn't feel anything in one place, but it feels rusty all over. The pain comes in and out. I don't know what that could be.

Coach Cal could feel Paul's split attention. He said, Have you gone over and congratulated your teammate yet?

Which one?

From his knelt position, Coach Cal fixed Paul square in the eye, like he could see through all his conceit.

Felix.

Paul felt a dagger in his pride.

Did you hear? Cal went on, He broke the course record today with the fastest time in the state this year.

Two daggers. Three daggers…

No, Paul said.

No what?

No, I haven't said anything. I will.

Coach left him alone with his rusty ankle, and Paul sat there and sat there, and listened and listened on his throne of ice.

When he did move he was careful to show that he had pulled something, tweaked something, and that he was so absorbed in its effects he was oblivious to the victor.

He hobbled around and muttered to himself and remained on the outside of the team gathering. Sam waved him in, to come closer, but Paul pointed at his leg and made a cringe to show he was tending to his injury. That the injury was serious.

Now there was a tradition after that race that Paul forgot about. It did not have an actual name, but the gist of it was that the lucky runner got pantsed, and had to give something like a pep talk press conference to the team.

How this all began no one knew, and it was never discussed formally. Like all great traditions, like all great impulses, it just happened. The when and where no one could say.

Felix knew none of this. He was in good spirits, aglow with his outstanding win and bouncing among his enthusiastic team. Other coaches and even the hot headed Duprees came up to him afterwards to offer their congrats, and when the crowd thinned he went off to the cooler to grab a gatorade.

Kirby quickly got all the attention of the team. All right? Are we doing this? There was a unanimous nod among them, among all but Paul, who remained apart, listening but feeling his leg.

They moved swiftly. Kirby came with the ice jug and Tits would do the pantsing. Dave was responsible for the distraction and Sam was an eager onlooker. And all of them had their phones armed and ready.

They were set. Felix cracked a fresh orange Gatorade. That's when Dave came up to him and said, Hey Felix, did anyone ever warn you about the Pants and Pep?

Felix looked at him confused. The what? Pants and pep? He raised his eyebrows and tipped back the bottle to take a big gulp. That's when they got him. First the crash of ice water, then the pantsing in quick succession. Then the gallery of cameras came out like they were snapping pictures, but they weren't. It was all part of the scenery, the improv stage they set, and the spotlight was on him.

He was shriveled, iced, buck as a jaybird. The Gatorade had splashed all over him, and it took him a moment of pure shock, as he stumbled over the icy carpet while using his hand as a fig leaf and trying to hike up his now transparent running shorts, to find his bearings. He pretended he was not hearing all the whistles and oohhs and ahhs as he was, raining from all sides, even beyond the walls of his team, who were good enough, decent enough to shield him from gawkers.

It was their own comedy show they staged and it was pure experiment because they had no idea how this poor newcomer would react to it. Hobble hobble, hitch hitch. They owww-

owwwed, they yeah babyed, they made cats meows. They said yeah jaybird, let It all hang loose. The whole thing had that distinct flavor of playful, homo manlove, that only a men's cross country team was capable of.

Like Marilyn Monroe above the air vent, Felix pulled up his see-through shorts and his face was red as red could be. Momo hopped around, making clicking motions with his fingers and ape sounds, a paparazzi ape.

Felix looked about ready to pop, or something. Team was about ready to relent, having delivered a fine dose, when Felix came into character of his own.

Antonio, he said, pointing his finger at the hopping paparazzi, Momo. My towel and my shades, por favor.

Antonio promptly went off and found the nearest towel and the nearest shades, which happened to be Dave's bleached pink towel and an unclaimed pair of discount store aviators. Both items flew at him, costume style, and he caught them out of the air, wrapped the towel around his waist and donned the shades.

Thank you, Antonio. Now that I'm properly clad, I feel like I can give my remarks.

He rubbed his thumb under his nose, raked his hand straight back through his hair, put his hands on his hips. He came forward to talk and the cameras turned to tape recorders.

Now Mr. Sun, any first remarks on the race today?

Mr. Sun leaned in. Indeed. The race went swimmingly, smoothly, serenely. Thank you, next question.

Mr. Sun, can you explain the orange glow coming off your face?

Are you referring to my succulent orange tinted mustache?

That is correct.

Well that is extremely personal, but yes I can explain that. That would be none other than Orange Gatorade, sir, which was gulped ravenously, and enjoyed heartily, prior to my knickers de-escalating. Thank you, next question.

De-escalating?

That is correct, next question.

Yes, Mr. Sun, could you tell us a little more about your secret cooldown regimen?

I can. And there's no secret about it. Steamy hot sauna, followed by a chilled glass of champagne and ice cold grapes.

Ice cold, Mr. Sun?

Excuse me, very cold. Very cold would be more accurate. Next question. Last question before I turn this towel into a whip.

Mr. Sun, Kirby said, reaching his tape recorder over the other heads. Can you give us any clue as to who you'll be bringing to homecoming this year?

Now this was a juicy question, and they all leaned in. Even Paul who was on the outside, pretending he was not listening, turned to hear what the answer was.

Mr. Sun lowered his aviators to the ridge of his nose so they could see his eyes, and fit them back into place. He flashed a subtle grin.

Next question, he said.

Mr. Sun, can you at least give us a clue? Can you affirm, there is someone you're taking to homecoming this year? A clue, just one clue, Mr. Sun. So we can wrap this interview up and you can get on to your ice cold grapes. Can we get a name? Can we get initials?

More silence, more sneaky grin from Mr. Sun. Mr. Sun took a step forward toward the outstretched microphones and itching ears. Then he whipped the aviators off and made a circle around his Gatorade mustache with his pointer and thumb.

He opened his mouth and closed it, keeping them in suspense. Then he stepped back, folded his arms, looked concerned, turned his head. He said Antonio?

Yes sir, Antonio replied.

Can I bum a cigarette?.

Of course sir, Antonio flicked him a fresh one when the front of his singlet and Mr. Sun lit it.

Now, said Mr. Sun. The name, the name…they want the name…

He stepped forward again, took a drag, blew a big imaginary puff in their eager faces. And when it cleared, he tapped the ash to the ground and said, Yes gentleman. I do have a name. And the name of my date is Sadie Press.

The Fourth Rule

Sadie Press. Let that name settle in a bit. At first they thought it was a joke, a funny, clever way to end an unexpectedly funny half naked press conference. Then it dawned on them. Felix Sun had broken the fourth, unspoken rule on the team: *Don't even think about Sadie Press.*

They had given this kid, this kid no one really knew that well, the stage and he swept it the way he swept the race moments before, in streams and strides. He was a ham, they saw, but was this a hoax? Was he really taking Sadie Press, *the* Sadie Press to the dance? And if so, how did that ever come to be? How did the kid who knew no one come to take out the untouchable Sadie?

The short and simple backstory is this: Sadie was Bill Press's daughter, his only daughter. She was a junior like Kirby and Tyson, and had been for most of her high school career, an All American runner, as you might expect with her dad being Bill Press.

She was also beautiful. She was the kind of intimidatingly beautiful girl that guys talked about in the locker room, but no one ever talked to in person - or, not for long because she had a way of making boys clam up.

That, and she was also never far from her father. Around Sadie, during those early years, Bill was Papa bear and Mama Bear put together. He had no problem showing his claws and sharpening his fangs if anyone got too close. And that included girls too.

In Sadie's freshman year at Loyola High, there was a senior by the name of Deborah Stills on the girl's team. She was a bold brazen Bohemian who bragged about being bi, and joked about how she was going to convert Sadie, who by then was already being called by some of her teammates, Miss America.

Rumors make a mess. And Press made a mess of that rumor by making a mess of Debbie Stills. One day that fall, after one of their practices, Press called her and walked her over behind his famous dirtbag car, which he parked in the corner of the lot under a pine tree. And there he chewed her out and lashed her down to a piece of shoe string and a heap of tears.

It was loud and people caught him calling her a lemon sucking hippie with devil's morals.

Whatever he said, however he said it, it worked. Without recourse to her own coach, or any of her teammates, she dropped the sport and stopped shaving her legs and started crusading around the school as a bona fide feminist, man hater, but eminently a Bill Press-hater. Her little burnout and brush with the Papa bear Press only served to enshrine his mystique as a no nonsense, no hippie bullshit, General Patton of the track.

A few months later Debbie came forward formally with accusations of discrimination and verbal abuse. But to her discredit, her team sided with Press, and they sided with Press because they sided with Sadie. They contradicted Debbie's claims with their own about her provocative locker room talk and how she made girls feel uncomfortable when they were dressing, etc.

The episode died there. Debbie continued to crusade and Sadie continued to run fast with a glow of admirers behind her.

By the end of her freshman year, she was the fastest girl on the team and one of the fastest girls in the state. Press knew her potential as he had known it since the time she was 5 years old and he had begun prepping her to be a prime athlete.

But he also knew his biggest challenge would not be knocking down the Debbie Stills of the world, but warding off the slobbery dogs who were his own runners, who simultaneously worshipped the track beneath Sadie's feet, and mortified of talking to her, about her, or looking anywhere near her while in Bill's company.

He knew all this, of course. He knew the way of boys, and he knew if things kept on the way they were going, someone was going to get burned.

The summer following her freshman year she transferred schools, to a Catholic all girls school called St Mary's, in the countryside, with a great running program.

The boys sighed. They cried. Howled at the moon that summer, when the drowning days had begun and there was no beautiful oasis, no running goddess passing them on the other side of the street or cruising along in red short shorts on the other side of the track.

Before the start of the season, Press asked the boys what their hopes were for the season, and they started by saying all the things he liked to hear about shutting up and showing up, about grinding and not quitting…

Then a hush came over them and he said, Anything else?

Dave, team funny man that he was, said, We were all wondering something, Coach.

The smile spread across the group of them sitting cross legged on the grass. They knew what he was thinking about.

And what would that be Mr Jones?

Dave started indirectly.

We were wondering what are the chances we run against some out of conference teams this year?

Such as?

Such as…St Mary's, for example.

Not one of them looked up to meet Press in the eyes. They all looked down. They shifted among themselves like a flighty flock of hens about to get a swinging boot.

I don't believe St Mary's has a men's running program, Mr. Jones. Sorry to disappoint you. Unless you might be referring to something else. You may have heard that Sadie goes there now. Where she'll no doubt have less… distractions… She didn't want to go, I can tell you that much, but I decided the best thing I can do for a girl like that is lock her in a castle till the right knight comes along. But I'll be long dead before then, he laughed.

That, or she'll be in the convent, making her vows. Hahaha. All right, enough of that. We've got one more round of intervals to do, so everybody to their feet.

Just like that they were up, shaking off their dead legs and Sadie fantasies. Press faced the track and set the whistle between his teeth.

Hey coach, Dave said a last time. Who's the dragon in the castle?

I'm the dragon, he smirked. The whistle rang. Now get to the line.

THE FOURTH RULE

* * *

On the bus ride back, the team up front asked Felix to explain himself. He told them Sadie was in his dance troupe, the one that met twice a week at Old Mill High. He said they were only friends, and not dating, and that he honestly didn't know her last name until he asked her to the dance and had to put her number in his phone.

Bullshit, called Kirby. This is classic. He's either just playing it down, or making the whole thing up. Give us some proof.

Felix showed them a picture on his phone of the dance troupe in the practice studio. He zoomed in to Sadie. All the guys up front hunched around the phone. Her hair was shorter, but that was her alright. The same stunning Sadie they remembered.

There's your proof, Kirb, Felix said.

Wait, why is she on the same dance team, or whatever it's called, as you? She's a runner too. She should be in season.

Yeah, she goes to St. Mary's, but she joined the dance troupe the same reason I did. Her school didn't have a program. And she's not running any more. She dropped the team this year.

Wait, what? Sadie's wicked fast. You mean she quit around the same time her dad quit coaching here?

I guess so, I'm not totally sure.

Damn, it's a weird world out there, Momo said. I wonder if there's a connection. What are the odds you show up here and she shows up there and…I can't wrap my mind around it. And you guys both dance? Does she know you run?

Yeah.

And?

And what?

Has she said anything about why she's not running or why her dad quit, or…

No, not really. The only thing she ever mentioned in passing is she said, 'Her mom's still getting over that'.

What's *that*? What was she referring to? Why Press quit?

Maybe, I don't know. Felix said. He shrugged and threw his phone back in his pocket.

Well what the heck are you doing, if you're not figuring out these details bro?

Kirby hit Momo on the knee. Hey Antonio, back off. I think what he's doing is working out pretty well for him.

Yeah, and what's that?

Getting a date to the dance.

That one stung. But it was a sweet sting. Antonio covered his embarrassed face with his hand, like he was trying to wipe the smile off. When he bounced up, he was still smiling.

Hey, you don't know I don't have a date. My date may not be as beautiful as Sadie Press, but she might be as voluptuous… that's a debate. But actually, I think you know my date pretty well, Kirby. I think you might've even had a thing for my date, back in the day, before you decided to 'upgrade' to Kara Klein…

He was toying with Kirby, trying to bait him into his joke, and Kirby knew it.

Are you done yet? Kirby said.

Alright, yeah I'm done.

Momo shoved back in his seat and threw his arm around Tits who had been listening over the back of the huddle.

Who am I kidding, everybody knows it's me and Titsy till the end. Cat's out. Here's my hot date boys, so don't be jealous.

We'll be there dressed to the nines, like we always are, with everybody saying, *Hey who's that handsome brown man and his fair skinned dime piece? Oh that's Antonio and Todd.* And then when they see the dance moves, don't even get me started on the dance moves. Don't think this ugly dog bite leg is going to slow me down on that account. We'll be coming in hot, right Tits? Doing our cha cha real slow, and then bouncing out when the fun's done to get ourselves some late night Taco Bell…because that's what we do…

He laughed at the vivid scene he was imagining. He shook it out of his head, shoved back into the middle aisle and tapped Felix on the knee.

You know I love hating on you, right Felix? You make me laugh. You're like my brother from another mother. You're like all our brothers from another mother. You know what I mean, Kirby? Isn't he? Thank goodness. Without you this season would be as serious as a funeral. Still feels that way sometimes. But then you go sweeping the race, calling me Antonio, being hilarious, being a dancer. Taking out Sadie Press without knowing it's the Sadie Press…life is crazy. It's crazier than the books…hey did you guys read Grapes of Wrath for English…

Tits elbowed him, said over his back. Yeah, some of us actually read it, Momo, and others googled half the sparknotes and skimmed the rest…

Pshh…anyway, I did read that book. Maybe not *all* of it, ok Tits, but most of it. And that book is boring as hell. Dustball this and that. What I'm trying to say is… this bus, you hooligans… he lifted off his seat and went round slapping the tops of their knees…These are *real* grapes, my friends.

The juicy grapes. These are the money grapes…it's what this season's meant to be about.

He glanced to the back of the bus, brought his voice to a whisper.

Even that grape back there. That big, sour griping grape, who never smiles any more, named Paul-stick-up-his-ass-Stafford - he's a grape too, in his own way. And I have no idea why I'm still talking about grapes. Wait, how did I get on grapes?

Can someone please hit him? Kirby said.

They jumped him. Tits hooked his elbows from behind, Felix and Kirby gave him titty twisters and Tyson joined the commotion, climbing over the seat and flicking his ears from above. Momo went down flailing, laughing, cussing in Spanish. He hated it and he loved it and he knew these were the grapes.

Paul, in his head

Paul had nowhere to take his losses or the news of Felix and Sadie, except into his head, where it wreaked havoc. He had that quintessential look of perfectionism. The inwardness, the isolation. The secret practices and burning showers. The distrust of others. The face that showed a broken smile when someone else was appreciated.

His once noble thoughts, his virtuous ambitions, his high mountain view of excellence - all of these crumbled and shrank to the size of a jail cell; a cramped space walled with jealousy and barred with resentment and shut out from light of good humor.

In running, as in all athletics, perhaps in all human domains, there is a punishment that leads to reward, an excellence bought with discipline. But there is also a punishment that leadeth unto more punishment, and a discipline that bears the rotten fruit of despair.

For the first time in his high school career, Paul ate the fruit of despair. He saw in his losses something more than reality. He saw a vision of his own self-created hell. Of years of self-affliction, of carefully upholding standards, and obeying the law of Press to the letter. Of slowly cutting himself off from his early friendships and alliances, from good-natured laughter and friendly gossip, teasing the girl's team and sitting on the cab of Dave's truck comparing blisters.

All of that felt distant. For days leading up to homecoming, Paul punished himself by locking himself in this spiderwebbed state of mind. He puzzled over the cruel enigma of Felix Sun. Felix Sun was not merely an affront to him. He was an affliction. He was the blank on the test, the D on the report card, the source, or rather the trigger of that deep-seated anger welling up within him.

What did one say about Felix Sun? He was not smart, rich, or particularly handsome, but lord in heaven he could run. There are a thousand ways you can describe a good runner. Some are like thoroughbred horses. They ripple with speed and power. They pound the dirt. They have a formidable presence of body. Others are like V8 engines. They rumble with intensity. They remind you of spark and gas, their arms and legs flying up and down like pistons. They press the pedal and they go. With more they get more.

But Felix Sun was different. Once in a while a kid comes along who sweeps hard work off the floor. Makes it seem like a dirty word to be used at all. Felix was like that. He ran like a hawk that fell from the sky. With a sudden, silent, devastating speed. He had a quicksilver stride, a reckless ease. He covered the earth with haunting swiftness, like the shadow of a passing cloud.

His secret was not effort, but *release*.

When they first met him they did not know this. They assumed he was just a pack runner. A fluff runner. He blended in and seemed to show nothing of exertion on his face. He barely sweat. Unlike Paul, he wore nothing on his sleeve. But run by run, they saw more of him. Running chiseled away the mystery of Felix. It released his humor and silliness. It revealed the man. His personality shone through. That season, Paul was the opposite. Running concealed him. He hid behind his records, hid behind his scholarship, hid behind his role as captain, and perhaps expected to hide behind them forever.

Both were talented, both were fast, but any close observer could spot the difference. Paul ran from something. He was always trying to outrun his fear of being caught, his need to impress coaches and win a scholarship. He was at war with time. Time was always burning too quickly, always in short supply. When he ran he heard a ticking in his head that grew louder as he went faster; a steady thock-thock-thock that swung back and forth evenly like a metronome.

What did Felix think about when he ran? What does someone hear in their head, who runs like that?

After Dover Sands, there was no rivalry really. Paul fell from his throne and Felix ascended. He ascended because he ran and he ran well. He ran like lightning on the heels of Kirby's thunder. He slipped all the surly bonds of controversy, of gossip and quarrel, of the whole entrenched prehistory of Press. Felix seemed to enjoy his talent the way a child enjoys sand at the beach. It flowed in, filled his bucket, and flowed out. With Paul it flowed in, stayed in, and turned rank.

By homecoming, Paul's mind settled to a single bitter truth. He was beat. He knew that much. It was one thing to be beat. It was another to be beat by a guy who didn't care that he beat you. That's what crushed him.

Homecoming

There was nothing more magical, nothing more wholesome and uplifting than Kirby Spence on homecoming night. His immaculate outfit shimmered on the hanger in the steamy bathroom where he was getting ready. Every few minutes his mother, who paced up and down the hallway, would press her face to the door and tell him to hurry up and don't use all the hot water.

From inside the shower, Kirby could only hear a muffled bickering outside, but he knew what she was saying. He knew the special inflections in your voice. *Kirby, don't use alllll the hot water.*

Too bad, he thought, as he hummed and scrubbed and lathered up his big unruly mane with a pump of his mother's 'vitamin rich, high volume, extra sheen' shampoo. He never ever touched that shampoo. Most days he threw on the generic old spice and called it good. But tonight he needed something special. Tonight, he thought, I'm using *alllll* the hot water.

He got out, patted dry and spent the next ten minutes with the towel wrapped around his waist, doing his hair in the mirror. An orange canister of pomade sat on the top of the sink. He took a goop and worked it into his fingers. He wiped the mirror clean and pressed up close to the glass, sculpting and molding. He started talking out loud to himself, rehearsing a couple cool opening lines when he saw Kara for the first time.

You look really nice, Kara.

He said it two times over and watched the way he said it in the mirror. He didn't like it. His head nodded oddly, and what was that weird hand gesture thing he was doing? The one that looked like he was giving a class presentation?

No, he thought. No *'nice'*. Definitely no 'nice'. *'Nice'* guys finish last. No *'nice'*.

He fixed his do, then he tried another.

You look stunning, Kara.

Stunning? Really? That word just felt weird coming out of his mouth. Had he ever used the word 'stunning' before in his life. It's homecoming anyway. I'm not taking her to a ball. No 'stunning'. Stunning's out.

His mother banged on the door. Kirby Spence, Don't tell me you're still in there prettying up…

Geez, can you give me a minute? I'm still getting ready.

Why is it taking you so long?

It's not taking me long. It's only been ten minutes.

All right, but don't be doing anything too "out there". Like the year…

Here again, he knew exactly what she was going to say. Yeah, yeah, yeah, he thought… the year *'your brother wore that silly spinner bow tie and everybody made fun of him'*.

Kirby stepped back and grabbed the handle and pulled it firmly shut.

Got it, thanks Mom. I'll be out in a few.

Her little interruption threw him off his game. He checked his watch. He did need to move it. No more rehearsing opening lines. He decided he was going to go with *beautiful*. Kara, you look beautiful. Keep it simple. Try not to do the weird hand thing. Okay, got it.

After he fixed his do, he put on the money suit. That was the only fitting description for that thing. It was big, it was purple, and it shimmered from shoulder to cuffs, crusted with probably 2,000 sequins.

Kara wasn't kidding. It was a showstopper and this is what he was wearing. Black button down underneath. No tie (not trying to be too stuffy). Black slacks, and then the finishing touch, the alligator skin dress shoes. Which he had to order specially from ebay, from some Western apparel store in Utah.

The shoes were huge, even for him. Size 17. Olive and brown and muddy alligator yellow, with a square toe and by all means authentic. But comfy they were not. And since they were used, the traction on the soles was bald. He put them on and almost slipped right away. They were very *slidey*. Good for dancing. He hoped, he really hoped. When the whole thing was dazzling and ready to go, he threw a pair of six shooters at himself in the mirror and came out.

His mother saw him from the kitchen and made a beeline. She waved a dishrag through the air, like she was shooing away a fly. He was the fly. The first thing she said was, Oh no. Oh no, Kirby. No, no, no. You're going like *that*?

He looked at his mother. She had a look that could cut him down from his two feet of surplus height. She was small as a radish, but when she was angry, when she disapproved of something heartily, she turned to a raging, redfaced jalapeno.

Like what? Kirby protested. Yes, I'm going like *this*. This is what I'm wearing.

Kirby's dad was sitting on the couch reading.

Honey, she said. Look at this, look what Kirby's trying to wear to homecoming. It looks so...she wrinkled her nose trying to find the word. *Frilly...*

Kirby's dad tossed a glance back, went back to his book.

Let him go like that if he wants. You only got a couple years in your life where you can pull off something like that.

Mrs. Spence stood there, with her screw eyes going up and over the frilly getup covering her big ginger-haired son.

Really though, Kirby. Whose idea was this? Is it like a joke? One of the kids on the track team?

No, I told you, it was my date's idea.

Your date, huh? She folded her arms, shifted to her other leg.

Yes, my date. Who I told you about a few weeks ago, remember? Not that it matters anymore.

Remind me of her name.

Kara Klein, his Dad chimed in.

See, Kirby said, Even Dad remembers. If Dad remembers, there's no way *you* forgot.

She couldn't argue with that. She scuttled off somewhere and came back and said, So this Kara is the one that wanted you to wear this? She's not, you know, pulling your leg? She's not going to stand you up or anything is she?

She's definitely pulling my leg, but she's definitely not standing me up. This is what I'm wearing, and this is what I'm doing. Now I gotta get going.

He tried to step past her to get the keys to the car, but she blocked his way.

Tell me your plans. Where are you off to now?

Dinner.

With?

Kara, Felix, and Sadie.

Ok. Sadie? Sadie who? I don't know that name.

Doesn't matter, Mom. I'm going.

Dinner where?

Outback.

Are you meeting there?

Me and Kara are meeting Felix and Sadie there.

So that means you're...

Yes, I'm picking up Kara. Right now.

He scooted around her as she ran his plan through her mothermind.

Hey dad, where are the keys to the civic? Kirby called out.

They should be up there on the counter.

Oh no Kirby, you can't take the Civic, his mother said. You got to take the other car.

Oh come on, no. There's no way I'm taking that freaking...

Hey, watch your mouth.

I didn't say anything. But I *need* to take the civic.

No Kirby.

Why can't he? His dad asked.

Yeah, why can't I? What's the big deal?

She stuck out three fingers. Because it's out of gas, it hasn't been cleaned, and the registrations almost expired.

Oh, come on. You can't be serious. 'Almost expired'?. That is ridiculous Mom. I'll fill it up, I'll throw the crap in the trunk, and since the registration is still good, then...

No, that's final. You take the other one. I feel better with you in the other one than I do with you in the civic. The civic's too fast and I don't need you speeding along these roads. You don't know what drivers are going to be like tonight. All your brothers took the other one. And Kirby, she added with that soft, victorious tone coming into her voice, It's much *much* safer than the other one too. Can you do that for your mother?

He grumbled toward the door. Safe, he thought. There's that word I've heard a million times before. Safe, safe, safe. All his life. Safe, nice, safe, nice.

He whipped the keys around his finger and went out.

There it was. 'The other one'. That's what they called it in the family. But outside the family it went by The Dragon. It was a mystic blue minivan with a beige underside and a bike rack on back that was never used and never removed. It had about 350,000 miles on it. It got the name dragon because the engine was obnoxiously loud and sometimes during summer when it got hot, smoke tailed out of the hood like it was overheating.

It was the essence of lame. And without debate, it was the car Kirby Spence was taking to pick up his date.

He got in, turned the keys and brought the dragon to life. He put the car in reverse and turned his back to leave the driveway, then he stopped on the pedal when he heard his mom calling after him.

Wait, wait! she called.

He stuck his head out of the window, released the pedal and kept rolling, hoping she would just float away, and leave him alone.

I got to go, he said, I'm already late.

But he couldn't ignore her. He stopped, sighed, put the car in park.

Wait right there. The little woman jogged back in the house and came out with an armload of stuff.

Here, before you go, take all this, she said.

What is it? What's all this?

On one arm she had draped one of his dad's brown blazers.

She offered it up toward him and he pushed it away. I'm not taking that, he said. No way.

Are you sure? Just take it as a backup.

Nope, no way.

Kirby, you look like a carrot top John Travolta in Disco Fever.

So be it. That's what I'm going to do, that's what I'm going for.

All right, then at least take these.

Oh, what the hell (the word slipped)… Heck! he corrected. Sorry, what the heck mom. I got to go.

Just take it. And don't forget to text me your plans.

It all came into the window, one thing after another. Bottled water, a snack bag of chips ahoy, a big jug of hand sanitizer, a small hand sanitizer, pocket pack Kleenex, and a car phone charger.

My phone's already charged, he objected.

Take it.

There's already a charger in here.

Take it!

He took it. He took all of it but the dusty brown blazer (thank goodness) And he was off. And he was late!

The dance

The dragon blistered down the main road before it pulled up to a line of traffic. The roads were busy that night. Kirby checked his phone and saw two messages from his mom already. One reminding him to text her his plans for the night, and the other, a long word paragraph of mother Spencer's cautions, don't, and careful. He did not read that message entirely, but he caught phrases. *Drive defensively... too wild... under the influence... no funny stuff... be decent.*

He could piece together the rest. He had six older brothers and all of them got the same rap at some point. But as the youngest he seemed to get it the worst.

Kara's text read, I'm ready, no rush.

He rushed. As soon as the traffic eased, he bobbed and weaved, as much as the dragon could bob and weave. He was frazzled, excited, nervous, all at once. Really nervous, actually. Maybe more nervous as he drove to her house than he was the day when he chickened out on the track.

He flipped the radio on, and keeping his eyes on the road, threw all the stuff his mom had thrown inside, to the back.

Kara's dad was a dentist in town, and they had a nice house on the other side of the main highway. Kirby parked on the curb and got out. He felt sweat drip from his neck down his chest. He took his phone out to text her that he was here, then he decided that was stupid. He put the phone away, and started up the sidewalk. When the door opened, he was caught momentarily in a patch of sun coming over the roof of the house. He put his hand out to shield the light, then stepped forward, out of the brightness.

All at once, she was right there in front of him. She had skipped down. A beautiful, brown-haired girl in a form fitting violet dress with a partial slit up the leg. She had heels on and her makeup done, and her mom and dad were standing on the landing behind them, waving.

Kirby waved up at the parents, gazed at the beautiful girl in front of him. He was flustered and self-conscious of being overheard in their presence. He faltered a little bit, Wow Kara, you look really, really *good*.

Although he said it with a big enthusiastic smile, the word *good* deflated in his head like a flat tire. *Good* was lamer than anything he practiced in the shower, lamer even than the dragon sitting on the curb behind them.

Kara waved her back at her parents, looped her arm through Kirby's, and off they went down the stairs.

Why thank you, she said. You look really really good yourself, Kirby. The jacket is just what I imagined, but the shoes really take it to another level.

When they got in the car he told her about ordering them off ebay, from the Western apparel store in Utah, and how the soles had no traction so she'd have to help him on the dance floor. He smiled, laughed, played along for those few transitional moments, but all he could think about was that klutzy opener. *Good*? Really *good*? Wow Kirby, that's what you opened with? For a girl like *that*? What happened to *beautiful*? Goodness gracious Kirby, pull it together. Look cool. Drive the dang car.

Her perfume, the glimmer of earrings, the cut of her dress and the way she crossed her legs so that one of her pretty legs glanced through the slit at him…woowee…he was about to reach back for one of those bottled waters.

It all caught him off guard. Girls at school didn't wear dresses that often. Not like that. They didn't doll up very often like that either. And they certainly didn't do all that and proceed to hop in Kirby Spence's family minivan either. It was too much for the big guy. Too much.

There was probably more woman in that car at that moment, than had ever been (no offense, mom). And he felt both honored and intimidated by that fact. His hands gripped the wheel tightly.

Kara held on to her seat, Do you always drive this fast? she said. You're really cooking. Are you already jazzed up and ready to hit the dance floor?

He chuckled, released his hands some. I guess I am, I guess I am.

The whole way there he was sweating generously under three pounds of sequins, but he got them to Outback, where Felix and Sadie had already gotten a table. That helped too. The sight of the other couple took some pressure off him, which had grown from the moment he bolted out of the house to the moment he was suddenly smitten in the presence of his 'really, really good' looking date.

* * *

He was so tall, even in the dragon. He was pressed for legroom. His legs bowed out at either side of the steering wheel as he drove. He looked like a big kid driving a toy truck.

Felix wore a classic black suit and blue tie that matched Sadie's dress. When Felix saw Kirby, he almost spat his water out. He went up to the big guy and passed his hand down the front of Kirby's money jacket.

Dude, he exclaimed, you didn't tell me you were going for best dressed tonight.

Kirby said, I feel like you and I are switched. You're the guy who comes in with Hawaiian shirts and tropical pants. And here you are looking like a class act. And here I am - he glanced down at his jacket, swayed it side to side for effect -

…Wearing purple thunder, Felix said, completing the thought.

They laughed.

Exactly, wearing purple thunder…

My friend, only you could pull that off. Honestly, he said as they rejoined ladies in the booth, I'm a little bit jealous. You're killing it. And the shoes too. I didn't even see the shoes. Wow. Watch out, people, Kirby Spence is pouring on the hot sauce tonight.

It's all her, Kirby tipped his head as he slid next to Kara in the booth. She's the brains behind the purple thunder.

They sat down and ordered food. They talked and told stories, One couple on each side of the booth. More couples and groups from their school filed past them. Halfway through dinner, most of the excess nerves Kirby had brought with him to the restaurant, had disappeared into the fun time they were having.

What he liked most of all is that they did not talk about

school, or running, or any of the usual fare track kids talked about; like meets, schedules, workouts.

They also never talked about Bill Press.

If Kirby hadn't known the girl sitting next to Felix was Bill's daughter, he never would have guessed it by her manner and look and conversation. All dinner long she had soft, smiling eyes, and a wide, open expression on her face. Like she was taking it all in, absorbing all the embarrassing stories about childhood pets, and enjoying it, really enjoying it. Even though she hardly knew these people, and even though, in a way, they hardly knew one another.

Maybe that was the magic, or part of it. The pomade and the purple thunder. The makeup and the updos. The prospect of the starry night ahead of them, and seeing their friends dressed up in the same way. That it could transport them so far out of their usual context, it was like discovering new people.

While they were on the topic of childhood pets, Kirby told the story of his pet turtle, Samson. Samson was a hand me down, turtle, he said. When you're the youngest of seven boys, you get a lot of hand me downs. Samson was no exception. Before me it belonged to Carl, and before Carl it belonged to Dan, all the way up the line to Jesse. I was three years old when I got Samson. It was the biggest day of my life. I remember that day. I cleaned my room and made my bed extra neat. To show that I was on my best behavior and responsible enough to take care of the turtle.

Carl brought him in, in his terrarium, and set him on the desk in the corner of my room. He plugged in the heat lamp, then he told me the only instructions I ever heard regarding Samson. He said, Don't touch him. Never touch him. Why, I asked, and Carl said, without missing a beat, Because Samson is the world's oldest turtle. And he's very angry because he's so old, and he'll bite you if you touch him, or even try to touch him.

Naturally, I swore I'd never touch him, and I didn't. Carl said I could feed him whatever I wanted. Even Cheez-Its. Which I did.

But he didn't eat those. He didn't eat anything. He didn't move. I asked Carl one day why Samson didn't move and he said, It's because he's really old. He sleeps a long time, like grandpa. It's called hibernating.

Carl was three years older than me, which made him six, and he blew my mind with that word. Hibernating. At one point, one of my brothers, I don't know which one, or when they did it - snuck into my room one night and moved Samson from one side of the box to the other. When I woke up the next day, I was so excited. I told all my brothers that Samson moved.

Weeks and weeks passed. Every night, I went to sleep with that red heat lamp on, whispering, Night-night Samson, hope you get more good sleep tonight, buddy.

And I meant it.

Then one day my dad came into my room. I think he was angry at Carl for some reason, but I don't know. He said, Kirby, Samson's gotta go.

I was devastated. I started crying. I said, I didn't do anything. I've been taking care of him like Carl said.

He looked into the terrarium. He said, Are these Cheez-its in here?

I said, Yes, because Carl told me…

But before I could finish what I was saying, he cut me off.

And he said what is now a very famous expression in our family. He said, Kirby, *You don't feed Cheez-its to a rock*.

I was baffled. I had no idea what he was talking about. And he could probably read that in my expression. But he reaches in and takes out Samson, the world's oldest turtle. The turtle I was told never to touch. He puts it in the palm of his hand. He says, Touch that.

I poked it.

He says, That, Kirby, is no Samson. That is a rock. That is a painted rock. Say goodbye. I said goodbye. And he promptly threw it out the window into our backyard.

When the others were through laughing at the story, Felix said, You're not going to be moving like Samson on the dance floor tonight, are you Kirby?

Kirby sat back, musing on Samson one last time. He shook his head. Felix, he said, compared to you and Sadie, I'm pretty sure everybody's going to be moving like Samson tonight.

* * *

By the time they finished dinner it was dusk. They took a few pictures outside the restaurant, then drove separately to the school. The parking lot was filled when they got there, so they parked in the neighborhood over and walked on. Kara looped her arm through Kirby's again and she pulled them along quicker when she heard the music pouring out of the open gym doors and saw groups and other couples making their way ahead of them.

From the parking lot they could see the silhouette of teachers outside the gym collecting tickets, and laser lights strobing inside. Kirby got three double takes and two compliments on his purple thunder before they got to the main doors. Even still, the nerves were coming back.

They handed their tickets over and came into the gym transfigured. The hoops were lifted and the bleachers stowed. Acres of silver streamers and gold ribbons and banners and twinkle lights spangled the ceiling, and walls and doorways. It's like the stars had come out inside. The lights from the DJ stage threw more color, more stars, more smoke. Pop song mashups thudded the shiny hardwood floor, and that's when Kirby got the first taste of his Wild West shoes. He slid everywhere. It was like walking on oil.

Kara got hold of him on one of his slips. You alright big guy? He said, I'm good. My kicks are just getting warmed up for the dance floor.

A couple of track girls called out to Kara, and she hollered back, tugging Kirby along. At each stage of the night, Kirby reached a point where he realized he had no map telling him where to go, or what to do. Among a group of pretty girls dressed up like that, one on his arm and the others tilting their heads back to take in his big, ginger, shimmering purple, alligator-skinned presence, he surely had no map. He had no clue what to say, or how to stand, or how to look cool. So he chuckled. A lot. He smiled and chuckled and used his height to look around for any of his teammates.

Wham! they spotted him first. Momo slapped him on the rear and Tits tapped his shoulder and ducked the other way. They gave the big guy a high five, and Kara paused from her girls to say hi.

How are you guys? Good to see you - Momo, right? Turning

THE DANCE

to Tits - she worked her lips together and said, And I know your nickname too, but I'm just going to go with Todd, since I'm not one of the guys.

That's great, Tits said. It's actually nice to hear my real name once in a while.

Momo said, Kara, I'm sure you already heard this tonight, but I must say, you look absolutely stunning tonight.

She placed her hand above her breast, dipped her head a little. She was taken by the compliment.

Well thank you, that's really, really sweet of you to say.

It might have been sweet for her to hear, but it was like vinegar on a wound for Kirby. *Good, good, really, really good.*

Karaf nudged Kirby, leaned into him playfully. She said, The big guy's my accessory tonight.

Yeah, he's something, isn't he, Tits said.

Both he and Momo were giving Kirby the eyes. Not that Kirby could read the eyes.

Hey, you catch up with them, she said, and I'll catch up with these gals, and we'll find each other in a couple minutes. Sound good?

Sounds good, Kirby said.

And off they went dragging the big guy, giving him grief.

* * *

Tits and Momo dragged Kirby over to the table of food and drinks. They posted up in a place where they could take in the whole gym. Kirby put his hands in his pocket, shook his head at Momo.

177

What's that look for? Momo said.

I hate you right now, Kirby smiled, but was also kind of serious.

You hate *me*? Don't even. We both hate *you*. Why do you hate me, what'd I do?

Compliment Kara,

What, I can't compliment?

No, it's not that.

What is it then? Come on, spit it out.

All day long I was thinking how I wanted to compliment her when I first saw her. Knowing that, you know, me and smooth words and girls haven't always gotten along together.

Yeah, I'm getting that right now. What did you say?

Kirby winced a little bit. I told her she looked *good*.

Like good, just good?

Well, I said you look 'really, really good'.

Momo bust out laughing. He spun around and had to cap his mouth with his hand.

That's like even worse than good just by itself. 'Really really good'? Hahaha… You are such a white boy. You gotta get some brown skin, Latino lessons in smooth talking in that big old head of yours. Yeah, OK, gotcha. Now I get it. Well, your solution is simple. Just redeem yourself…compliment her again. Before the night is up. End on a high note. You can only go up from *good*. If you want, I can even send you a couple Spanish phrases I guarantee you she hasn't heard in Spanish class before. Something to slip in there when you're taking her back and the moods just right, and your hands on her…,

All right, I get your point, now you're making me uncomfortable.

That's the point bro. That's the place you wanna be...you want that shaking in the knees, that's a good thing. Now can we cut your problems in perspective and tell you the real issue, why we hate *you*, big boy...? Because while you're over there feeling nervous, beating yourself up for not saying your beautiful words just right - you're missing the fact that you got a girl, hoss! And I got, you know - he thumbed back - stunning Tits.

Hey, what's that mean? Tits said, trying to get into the conversation.

Momo edged him off, continued explaining to Kirby.

And while you were over there, getting swarmed by the gorgeous girl squad tonight, we were back here for 20 minutes eating celery and hummus. I looked back at one point and Tits is catching up with Miss Allen, who's chaperoning tonight, and they're talking about the AP Calc exam study session. So do you feel my pain Kirby? This is what you get with Tits. And he also happens to be wearing a pair of *my* boxer briefs tonight because we got ready together and guess who forgot to pack some for himself? So, there you go, Mr. 'really, really good.' How's that for perspective? You can take all your troubles, and... he put his hands together and made like he was tearing a paper to scraps, letting the scraps snowflake all over the floor.

Tits puckered his lips. You know you love me, Momo.

Yeah, and I love you both, Kirby said. Now, moving on, I'm going to get some grub.

He turned but Momo caught him by the cuff, and raised his brows suggestively.

First, some punch, Momo insisted, with an emphasis on the word punch. Then he produced from the folds of his suit, or from somewhere, an innocent looking red beverage in a clear plastic cup.

Punch? Kirby took it hesitantly, brought it up to his nose.

Momo produced his own cup, and Tits the same.

Don't even ask, Momo said.

Together they lifted their cups in the air.

Momo raised the toast.

To smooth lips, and a really really good time tonight…

They sipped. They smiled. Whatever they drank hit in the back of the throat, and went down smooth.

Punchhhhh.

* * *

Throughout the night, the group joined and rejoined. Kirby caught up with Kara, and Momo and Tits found Sam and Dave. Later they found Tyson. They found Felix and Sadie, and the men's team and the women's team formed a big group on the dance floor. The only person no one saw for a long time was Paul. Eventually, he appeared, but it was hard to recognize him at first, because he was wearing sunglasses. He hung out exclusively with the football team, and made no attempt to see his own. With the exception of Sam and Dave.

As the dancing picked up, Kara took her heels off and asked Kirby to hold them in the pockets of his suit jacket, while she put on her dancing flats. After that, Kirby's pockets bulged at the side and he had to be careful not to swing too fiercely around and club someone with the shoes.

On any other night, Kirby might've been content to do his basic knee bounce and side to side. And the hands. The hands were always an issue. Sometimes they flopped at his side, like he was patting down his pockets, looking for car keys. Sometimes they strobed in the air, fingers opening and closing, like his hands were two flashlights, turning off and on. Whatever the moves were called, they were trademark Kirby; the same, safe, tinman dance moves he did at every dance.

That night though, with his team and Kara around him, he opened up a little bit more. His hips loosened, started going side to side, round and round. That was novel. Kirby hips never went to side to side or round and round. He began to take more liberty. He had a wave of confidence post-punch and post all the things Momo told him about being the one guy surrounded by all the girls. It put some swagger in his step. Kara encouraged it too. The more she saw him trying something new, the more she cheered, and the more he heard the voices around him, saying, Get it Kirb, get it!!

He was getting it, and it was getting him. The ironic thing about the alligator skin shoes is that the bald bottoms added a precarious swivel and swerve to his moves. His feet were unpredictable, and his unpredictable feet made for good dancing. He would return to one of his safe moves when suddenly a shoe would shoot out from under him and his whole body, including the purple thunder would catch the slide. People thought this was him dancing. him coming alive like disco fever John Travolta. The more he did it, the more Kara and his teammates owwwed and ahhhhed and hammed it up for him.

At one point he nearly wiped out bad. He spun on his heel all the way around, his arms noodling and flailing for someone to grab hold of. Kara caught him at the last moment in the position of a dip - her dipping him. There was a big cheer. He had no idea what he did. All he could see was her surprised face and a loose lock of her brown hair, looking down at him, and the twinkling lights on the ceiling above her.

He should've been embarrassed, but he wasn't. Not even slightly. When he got to his feet, he did something else he never planned on doing, and never saw coming. He kissed her. It was a cheek kiss, but it was a kiss nonetheless. He could smell the makeup on her face. He did it so quickly, and so instinctively it sort of stunned him, in a good way.

The next song he consciously reined in all his sprawling moves, and when the song was over the two of them went off and took a break. They got snacks and found a pair of fold up chairs away from the big crowd. They sat eating for a while, not saying anything, just people watching. She pointed at his plate with a tip for her carrot stick, and he held it out while she dipped in his ranch.

Finally, she said, So…

So…

You had some pretty smooth moves out there, Kirby.

Without looking at her he could see the smile in her eyes and hear the pause between the words. He noticed the way she said 'moves', when she really meant 'move'. *The* move. The thing that happened back there in front of all her friends.

With a little chuckle, he put his wrist to his mouth as he finished swallowing. Then he said the smoothest thing he had said all night.

Blame it on the jacket.

* * *

THE DANCE

It was marvelous to watch Kirby Spence on his game that night. His teammates saw it. Everybody saw it. And no one quite expected it. That was the beauty of it. It was like the kiss. It was a surprise.

Kirby was one of those good salt of the earth boys with so hardnosed a mother and so much repressed romance in his tall, gangly, shy, deep-voiced body - it had nowhere else to go except into some athletic pursuit. All of high school, maybe all his life he either left it burning in his heart or burning on his heels. But that night he left it burning everywhere. In every dance, move, in every conversation. In every smile and chuckle. He was like a lamp with the shade removed. He beamed. It was not just because of Kara, though she was a big part of it. There was so much love in his heart. For that time, and that place. For those people, and that punch, and that Momo with his jokes, and that Tits with his world-class gooberself talking to Miss Allen. Love for Felix and Sadie and for his mom and her twenty questions. There was all this love in Kirby Spence, and it was flowing out.

There was even love for Paul Stafford. Paul. Big Paul. Paul, with his ridiculous shades on, loud and jumping around with the big football boys. Oh Paul, Kirby thought when he saw him from across the hall.

During one of the songs, a circle formed around Félix, who began to break dance on the floor. A loud chant echoed across the gym. Fe-lix Sun! Fe-lix, Sun! At the same time the chant began, Kirby, who could see over everybody, saw Paul retreat from the big crowd to the lonely fringe of the dance floor. After the dance, the team stormed Felix. The following song was one of those club hits where the beat builds and builds, and then drops. At the beat drop the whole team minus Paul jumping up and down, shoving one guy in the middle back-and-forth, getting louder and louder. Felix was that guy in the middle.

Between the mayhem, and the laughter and the dancing, Kirby kept seeing Paul. He was not looking for Paul. But he kept finding Paul and the corner of his vision, standing off by himself.

One of the last songs that night was a slow dance. Half the dancing crowd dispersed. All but those with dates remained on the dance floor. Kara found Kirby's hand and led him into the middle of the floor. And he wrapped his hands gently around her, clasping them on the small of her back. He had to lower his head quite a bit for her to reach her arms around his neck, but he was more than happy to do so. They danced. Their heads were so close together their foreheads touched and Kirby could feel the sweat on her skin from all their dancing. He released her and gave her a twirl. As she was twirling in, Kirby could see Momo and Tits shuttling one of the silver decoration balloons back-and-forth like a football. Kirby laughed. Kara came in and whispered something so close in his ear he felt a shiver go down his back.

What are you smiling about?

Nothing, he said.

Are you sure?

I'm sure. Only thing I'm smiling about is having a great night with a great date.

As they danced, they bumped into Sadie and Felix, by accident. Felix gave Kirby a wink, and Kirby returned it. Dave and his girlfriend swayed by, and Dave said, Boys, I think we're making history tonight. Between the three of us and Tyson, we've got four cross country kids on the dance floor during a slow song. And they're all dancing with girls. Now *that* is a record.

The couples laughed, floated their separate ways, and when the song ended, Kara and Kirby stepped off the dance floor. Kara said, It is funny what Dave said. I remember last year, a slow song came on and all of you guys came out together and danced with one another.

Yeah, Kirby said, I'm glad those days are done.

Are they though? Why are cross country guys always so… Touchy-feely?

Exactly!

It's a mystery. I've been part of it for years and I still don't get it. It's just the way it is.

And to think it was almost five of you out there tonight too.

What do you mean, five?

You didn't hear? What happened to Paul?

No, what?

Paul asked out my teammate Bethany Clayton at the last minute and it didn't go well.

Oh, really? What, she turned it down?

Partly. She did turn him down. Someone had asked her out weeks ago. But apparently he took it bad. He cussed, punched a wall, made her feel horrible. And Bethany is like one of the sweetest girls on the team.

I didn't even think they knew each other, Kirby said.

Yeah, that's the thing. That's what made it so traumatic for her. She told us she basically only ever talked to him like two times before. And then he asked her out of the blue and chewed her out for already having a date. It didn't really sound like Paul, but I guess he snapped.

Yeah, well this year has been hard for him. Hard for all of

us on the team actually.

Sorry, Kirby. I didn't wanna throw a wet blanket on the dancing. It just came to my mind.

I understand…Speaking of, he gave her a look, and they dropped the conversation.

Paul crossed behind them.

Kirby said Hey, and Paul brushed past him without a word.

In his head, Kirby tried to leave the matter alone, but he couldn't. He had already been thinking about Paul, even before Kara mentioned the episode with Bethany. Now it nagged him more. The music was going again, the last few songs. Time to finish strong. But Kirby kept hearing a little voice in his head that said, *Find him, find him…*

The little voice insisted. The music couldn't drown it out. Not even Kara, beautiful Kara, jumping in and calling for him to join her, could stop the little voice from chiming in his head, *Find him, find him.* Kara swung her dance lasso out and started pulling him in, when again, Kirby caught Paul in the corner of his eye. Paul was leaving. Kara pulled and tugged, but Kirby hesitated, frozen at the edge of the dance floor. He looked down at the tops of his big alligator shoes, then he placed his finger in the air, and started jogging the other way, threading through the crowd. Kara's lasso fell to her side. She stared at him, confused. What he was doing. I'm sorry, he called back. I gotta do something. Real quick. I'll be right back.

He ran out the main doors, looking for Paul. From the top of the concrete stairs he looked out over the full parking lot and saw him a good ways out, moving quickly. Kirby hopped down the stairs, calling his name. He could see the double blink of a car in the corner of the lot.

Paul! Paul!…

No reply.

Kirby picked it up. He could feel the cool night air blowing on his face, and hear the crunch of his shoes on the sidewalk and feel his thousands of sequins and two heels on either side of his jacket swinging back-and-forth.

He ran with urgency. But he did not know why exactly. He did not know why he felt compelled to track down Paul, who had ragged on him all year and ragged on him all of his high school career. The small voice that tempted him out of the dance to go find Paul was now tempting him to turn back and let Paul do whatever he wants. He proceeded, but it felt like a tug of war between his head and his heart. He slowed up when he got within eyesight of the car. The car idled. Paul sat in the front seat, his face illuminated by the blue light of a phone screen. It was a black BMW sedan, Paul's dad's car.

Watching him under the blue light from his phone, Kirby noticed something else about Paul that unsettled him. Paul had taken his sunglasses off and his eyes looked strange. They looked swollen and darkly red. Kirby thought maybe it was a trick of the light, but the closer he got the more pronounced the swelling appeared. They looked worse than sickly. They looked haunted. Stricken. Burned out. Like they had been staring into the sun.

Paul saw Kirby before Kirby had a chance to speak up. Paul ditched his phone and abruptly snapped his sunglasses on again. Kirby waved. He stepped off the curb and came over to Paul's car.

What's going on, Paul said. What are you looking for?

Kirby came over to the passenger side. He put his hand on top of the car and lowered his head. He said, I guess I was just coming to check on you.

Check on me? Paul scoffed. Does that make you a chaperone then?

Paul flicked his phone on, like he was checking for a message. Then he flicked it off. Kirby removed his hand from the top of the car and stuffed both his hands into his back pockets. He felt awkward and embarrassed to be talking to Paul, or trying to talk to Paul.

You got something in your jacket? Paul pointed.

Kirby patted his side pocket and pulled out Kara's high heel, which made him smile. He showed Paul, hoping it might help break the ice some, but Paul gave no sign that he thought it was funny. Kirby continued to feel like this was a mistake, coming over.

Kirby said, We were all just wondering where you were. Me and the guys, while we were in there making a fool on the dance floor.

You and the guys, really? That's a funny way to put it. Fooling around, huh? I'm sure you were leading the squad on that account.

It was a statement that could have been said with humor, but Paul's delivery stripped it to a mean, purely mean, cut. Kirby could feel the conversation dying. Not just dying because there was nothing else to say, but being tortured with sarcasm. Shot down with snideness. Kirby did not know what to say. All his attempts to build a bridge to Paul were hazed in that critical spirit. He felt in those brief, frivolous replies, Paul's complete dismissal of him, and it hurt. He fought an urge to strike back, to tell the kid with the swollen eyes how pitiful it was he came alone, that he shamed Bethany Clayton, and himself, and that the dried cut mark above his knuckles proved it. He wanted to tell him that he had seen the zombie eyes, and go down the list, one thing after another - just unload on this self-centered, Oregon bound, horrible, worst version of Paul Stafford he had ever known.

But he heard footsteps behind him, and he took all his pity, all his rejected kindness, all the love that had been flowing through his veins that night - and stepped away from the car. He turned back the other way. His head dropped. He looked back once and saw that Paul had not even noticed he had left. His face was engulfed in his phone.

The love and hate swirled and Kirby's thoughts like sand in a windstorm. The little voice he heard when he ditched his beautiful date that said, 'find him', changed to another choice four letter word beginning with the letter f. F him.

Kirby was so lost in his thoughts he did not see the trio coming the other way. Three football guys who are also preoccupied and didn't see Kirby coming. The three of them were drunk as all get out. The two in front were walking forward but talking backward, with the third, a guy named Bryce fiddling with something in his hands.

Kirby with his head down and the three drunk boisterous boys collided, purely by accident. The two guys in front took the main fall. They were happy drunks, and profuse with apologies. They helped each other and the big guy up. It was Bryce, the one in the rear, fiddling with something, who was livid. Whatever he dropped partly sprayed over Kirby and scattered all over the dark sidewalk. It sounded like tic tacs or hard candy hitting the ground.

In a second, Bryce was on his knees cussing up a storm, pushing his two idiot friends away, saying get your feet off the effing sidewalk. So I can see where they went.

Kirby, sorry to run into them, and trying to be helpful,

turned his phone flashlight on and for a brief moment, three football drunks scrambled to collect their missing items before they realized who was helping them and what he was seeing.

Plastic baggies and dozens of pretty pink pills mired the sidewalks and the lines between. Many more hopped off the paved area into the grass.

Hey, Bryce yelled, to the light bearer behind him, Shine that over here more.

When he looked up to give his order that's when he realized who was pointing the light.

Oh shit! Get out, I mean, sorry, thanks we've got it.

He jumped in front of the bright circle of light and used his wide football shoulders to obscure what they were collecting on the ground. But by then Kirby had seen what he had seen. He stepped away as if he saw nothing. Played dumb. Behind him he heard a car door open and close. Bryce said, The hell are you doing just sitting there, while we're over here trying to get this up before…

Kirby walked slowly in the dark, with his head forward but his ears back. He didn't make out Paul's soft reply. But he heard Bryce say, Well come on. Help us sweep up. These little shits are pricey. And it's your stash anyway.

End of the night

Those were the last words Kirby heard before he re-entered the gym. The dance was over. Background music was playing from the dj booth and a few of the overhead lights had come on. Chaperones were folding chairs and the big crowd was filing out of the double doors into the cool fragrant night. Couples were hanging on the rails, laughing, talking after party plans.

He looked frantically for Kara. He found her standing with Bethany Clayton and her date near the exit. He apologized for leaving the way he did. Told her he'd explain when he took her back.

With a bit of disappointment in her voice, she said, It's all right Kirby. I understand if you want to stay out with your guys. I asked Bethany if I could get a ride with them. It's no problem if you want to split up tonight.

Split up, he thought. The phrase clashed in his ears. He gave a woeful look at his band of dumb, delightful teammates and sighed as he turned back to her. He was wearing his biggest, warmest puppy dog eyes. He said, Firstly, tell Bethany Clayton thank you, but no thank you. I'm taking you back, if you'll let me. Number two, I love those guys over there to death, most of them anyway. But I've had more than enough of them tonight. Way more. Number three, girls gotta eat. And you're my date tonight. So unless you're satisfied with carrots and red peppers, we've got some late night munchies to attend to.

Number four…number four was on the tip of his tongue, then he lost it. He folded his arms and knit his brows. He caught a glimpse of her looking up at him with shining fascination.

Oh come on, she said, steering him outside. You can think of number four. Right now, I'm more interested in number three. Girls gotta eat. So lead the way Kirby Spence.

They found a late night pizza joint and ordered a plain cheese pie, which they split. They flipped the box open on the center console between them and ate it in the parking lot as the dragon played old pop cds which Kara found in the compartment below her seat. A treasure trove of Backstreet Boys, Baha Men, Smash Mouth, Weezer, and R. Kelly. Real throwbacks. She asked which of his brothers owned which cd and he said, I have no clue. The only one I know for sure is the R. Kelly, because that one's mine.

Another hand me down?

Absolutely, he laughed. One of the few I was happy to get.

Really?…

Something made her laugh so hard she had to put down her slice and grab a napkin to wipe her eyes.

What is it?

Oh nothing. Just the thought of you a few years back bumping down the road in this van with your learner's permit, blasting hot and heavy r&b.

He took a bite, chewed and thought about it. That's a part of me most people never see.

It's a good part I'd say. She popped out the Smash Mouth that was playing and popped in the R. Kelly.

With a half-finished slice in one hand, she pulled a couple car seat dance moves, made a big yawn and leaned over against the side of the door.

You have any after party thoughts or plans? He asked.

She rolled her drowsy brown eyes toward him.

These are my after-party plans. Then, with a sweet smile she curled her legs up on the seat and drew little shapes on the window.

She was pooped. They both were. Maybe it was the pizza. Maybe it was the dancing. Maybe it was the R. Kelly. Maybe it was all of it.

As he drove her back she lowered the music. She said, Were you going to tell me what you were doing outside, when you left the dance?

It's not worth getting into, he said. That's a story for another time.

A good one or a back one?

I wish I could say, but it's not looking so good right now.

Kara searched around the car. In the backseat she happened to find among the pile of things his mother tossed back there, a snack bag of chips ahoy from earlier.

Oh! She exclaimed. I see you're holding out on me? May i?

Please do, they're all yours.

She gobbled a few cookies and started to laugh again.

What is it this time?

She pulled out one of the cookies and held up for him to see.

Guess what this reminds me of? Her eyes twinkled, wondering if he was on the same wavelength.

He grinned. Easy, he said.

Do you?

I do.

Well give me a clue. Mister read my mind.

He pulled up to her house. He put the van in park, turned the music off.

It involves me, for one.

Check, what else?

And my brothers…

Check, and…?

A beloved pet I used to own.

She whacked him. You knew?! How do you know I was thinking that?

I saw you take one out of the bag and smile, and I just knew.

The laughter in the car got quickly quiet. Kirby handed her back her heels. She hooked them around her fingers and looked out the window to her house. The lights inside were out. A porch light was on.

How do I end this date the right way, Kirby thought. For days leading up to homecoming he had seen all the various moments of that day play out in his mind pretty clearly.

Until now. He could feel the tension. The unspoken fever. This was that moment when kids made out, or made some move, and someone came by and knocked on the window.

But that wasn't it.

Kara put her hand on the latch and opened the door partly. She said, Thank you Kirby for a really fun day. I'm going to remember you and your outfit and dance moves for a really long time.

Thanks, he said. There was more he wanted to say, but he felt like he was clamming up. He put out his hand and caught hold of her before she left and gave her another peck on the cheek. It was nothing crazy, but that wasn't quite it either. As she got out and waved goodbye, he felt his heart begin to race and a lump in his throat. Come on Kirb, do something. Give it a little more gas. Felt like he was leaving something unfinished, something incomplete.

Without thinking he threw his door open and shouted, wait, his deep, nervous voice breaking down the quiet suburb street. She watched him as he jogged up the steps, breathless and wild-eyed.

The fourth thing. I forgot to tell you back there and I've been wanting to tell you all night, since I saw you. Frankly I got too nervous the first time I saw you. But here it is….

His hands pattered at his sides like a little drum roll, like he was working himself up to the words.

I think you're wildly, ridiculously, stunningly beautiful, and way out of my league, and um…

He stepped forward, lassoed her into his big arms and planted a big wet Kirby-sized kiss right on her lips. Then he released her.

She was amazed, startled, her whole face glowed. As quickly as he jogged up, he jogged back down to the dragon where the door was still flung open in the road. Over the top of the car he shouted one more thing: Like I said, blame it on the jacket. Then he hopped in, gave her two cute honks and headed off.

He drove like a wild man back to his own abode. He dropped the windows, let his hair shake out of the careful pomade mold. He worked his lips back and forth and all around. They were dumbstruck. They felt like gummy worms. He turned the old R Kelly hit, Remix to Ignition, way up - because it was hot and soulful and smooth, and it was exactly what he needed to hear right then. And he left the faithful dragon breathe its fire down the mild, sweet smelling night.

He parked and came up through the dewy grass and took a deep breath and exhaled. He opened the door. He removed his five pound sparkling jacket. Kicked off his aching, sliding, obnoxiously big alligator shoes.

He was sure Mother Spence would be up waiting for him, lurking in the dark corner of the living room, ready to tear him a new one. Ready to ask what that silly look on his face was for, and if he had been safe and responsible, and if he drove defensively, all the questions…

And furthermore he was prepared to tell her,

No Mom. I was not safe. Not by a long shot. And responsible can go kiss my ass. Yes, I said ASS. I lived it up. And I drove like a maniac. And I kissed the girl. And I told her she was stunningly beautiful. And I, Kirby Spence, six foot five wallflower, and youngest of seven ginger brothers, had the time of my life tonight.

He was ready to die on that hill of his big desire.

But when he came home that night, he did not find her there. She had gone to sleep. There was a light on in the kitchen, and to his surprise, a pan of walnut brownies covered over with aluminum foil and a sticky note on top that said,

Sorry didn't let you take the civic. Hope the dance was lots of fun.

(Heart) mom.

When her boys had a tough day, Mama Spence made food. Food was her olive branch. She apologized with food, mended wounds with food. She could be a tough one, but food was how she showed her tenderness.

Kirby cut two big slabs of brownie and poured himself a

glass of ice cold milk and went back to his room. He laid in his bed and played moments from that night over and over again in his head. He thought of Kara and her dress and her pretty face and her cute crossed legs and cuter dance moves. He thought of Paul and the pills. He thought of the sweaty gym and the twinkly light ceiling. He thought of his teammates. Of Tits and Momo slow dancing and Tits wearing Momo's briefs. He thought of Sadie and Felix and Tyson and Samson. And a dozen other funny moments.

And last of all he thought of that thing Momo said on the bus a couple days back. When he was talking too much. About how these were the best days, the days you look back on and miss. The days that are sweet, even when they're not sweet. The ones that leave a good ache in your heart. These are the grapes.

Kirby closed his eyes and he knew what that meant.

Poker night

The boys held a poker night the following week. Tits set it up and hosted it at his house, in the musty two-car garage with a sloping driveway. They passed a bottle of his dad's old beefeater under the table between hands. Poker night was something they had always done in years past, but hadn't kept up with the same frequency that year. It was Momo, Tits, Tyson, Felix and Kirby.

When Kirby arrived, the rest of them started whistling. Well it's about time the lover boy arrived, Felix said.

I'm surprised he's not dressed up in his hot purple blazer, after all the luck he was having with it on homecoming, Tits replied.

That wasn't the jacket, Tits. That was the Latin fever rubbing off on him, Momo added. Look at him, it's written all over his face. He's trying to play it cool, get into his poker face, but I can see right past it.

Kirby pulled up a stool and Tits dealt the cards. Texas hold'em, 20 bucks buy in. Tits was wearing a hideous pair of poker shades with holographic snake eyes on them. Kirby didn't say much when they began. He put his money into the pile and the first few hands went quickly. Tits and Momo raised one another and everyone else folded. It went on that way for the next hour, until the other guys were short of money. It was an unusual round because usually Kirby was in the mix with Tits and Momo. Tyson and Felix were self-professed scrubs, but the others played for blood. And week after week when they were playing regularly the three of them tended to split the spoils among them.

That night the game dragged on. Tyson bought in twice, lost it all, and bailed out. Felix had a bit of beginner's luck and raised Tits on a few hands and made him fold. Then he got cocky, overbet, lost his buy in and bailed.

Momo, who for most of his waking hours was a talking machine, got deadly silent and serious when it came to poker. He fancied himself a good read of people. Kirby, he thought, was either hot or cold tonight. And when he was hot, he ran the bets up and the three of them duked it out and stole everyone else's money. But that night something was off. He was reading something else in Kirby's face. Kirby looked dreamy, locked up in his head. He was untypically quiet and tame that evening, playing safe hands and folding early and hesitating about whether to buy back in or not.

As the game dwindled, with Kirby on his last dollars, Momo said, where have you been all night? Is this your slow play? Try and get Tits and I fat and happy and then pounce on us?

Kirby showed little emotion. A shade of a smile, maybe, but no chuckle. It was either a true poker face or there was something else going on.

He tapped for cards.

This big guy is bugging me out for real. His face looks like a storm brewing. Seriously man, jokes aside, you doing all right?

Don't listen to him, Kirby, Tits said. This is just part of Momo's smooth talking tactic. He's trying to throw you off your game. Keep doing what you're doing. It's working. And you both keep it up so I can steal all your money.

Kirby looked across the table at Tits. He said I'm going to raise the stakes some.

That comment halted the game.

Oh damn, now here we go!

Raise the stakes? What do you have in mind? Even though you've been powder puffing all game, now you want to up the ante? Momo nipped.

What do you have in mind, Tits said.

It's not on the table, Kirby said. Tits, you remember that thing you said you knew about Paul. That secret that if you showed him, it would break him?

I don't know if I used those words, but yeah I do. And yeah I have it. I have it here in this house. Why? What do you want with it? And what does that have to do with our game? I might have to agree with you Momo. This guy is acting fishy.

I want to use it, Kirby said.

Really, I wouldn't have pegged you for one to want to take down Paul Stafford for the hell of it.

It's not for the hell of it. But I do want to take Paul down. And I want all of you to help me.

Tyson had been lazy back in his chair, playing on his phone. Right away he sat up. This sounds like it's getting interesting.

Momo waved his hand through the air, protesting.

Hold on a sec. I'm confused. Are we still playing poker?

Games off, Kirby declared. Finally broke the icy expression he'd been wearing all evening. It was clear he had something on his mind, something he needed to get off his chest.

Sorry to spoil the fun guys. You can win my money next time, Momo. Tits, go get your thing, your silver bullet, whatever it is.

All right, give me a second. You guys grab yourself another soda and snacks.

He took off his holographic shades, left the garage and came back a few minutes later with an envelope, plain and unmarked. He flapped it in his hand before tossing it into the middle of the table. Felix scooted in and cleared away the mess of cards and poker chips.

There you go, he said.

Right, so it's a plain envelope? Looks like…? Tyson said.

Guys, take a look at Tits right now, Momo said, drawing their attention to the sly grin on Tit's face. The slightest bit of power goes right to his head…

Tits snatched the envelope off the table.

I'm not letting power get to my head. This letter here isn't really power, per se. It's what I like to call good old-fashioned blackmail.

And were you planning on using it? Tyson asked.

So it's a letter? Momo laughed. Did anyone else hear that slip? What kind of letter?

Wait! Tits put the envelope behind his back. His eyes cut left and right, guarding his prized possession.

Hey, before anything happens here, how about we keep our eyes on the ball and remember, it was this guy - he pointed the envelope at Kirby - who had the idea, who called off the game and started making big talk about Stafford. What do you got Kirb? You must have something.

Yeah I agree. This must be pretty serious unless this is a big bluff, but I doubt it.

Kirby pulled his stool up to the table. Then he reached in his pocket and pulled out his own prize possession. Whatever it was, he held it in the cage of his hand, not letting them get an early peek, building the suspense. He shook his hand like he was warming up dice, then he tossed them over the green surface, five pink pills, oval shaped and dotted with copper colored glitter. They skipped to all corners of the table.

Oh shit, someone said.

They all leaned in to take a closer look.

I second that, Momo said. His eyes were fixed on the tiny objects.

It so happened, the moment they shot out of Kirby's hand onto the table, all the hands around the table drew back, like a knee jerk reaction to something dangerous.

Tyson was the first to make a move. He rested his elbows on the edge of the table and one of his hands stepped down. He grabbed a pink jewel from hiding inside the edge of the table. He brought it in front of him, spun it in place with the nail of his pointer, as if it were another poker chip. Then he flipped it to the other side of the table where Tits did the same thing. As he was picking it up, his mom walked into the garage with two heads of iceberg lettuce. She opened the second fridge. The boys froze, said not a word.

I'll be right out guys, don't worry, I'm not trying to get in your game. They sat stapled to their seats.

On her way out she turned in the doorway and said jokingly, I hope you guys don't get that quiet around every girl.

It was a close call. Not that Tit's mom had any idea what they were doing, or that if she had come over and put her eyes on the table she would have been able to identify the pills as glit. But up until that point, no one had even said that word.

It was a dirty word, a dangerous word.

Does everyone know what this is? Tyson asked. He looked around.

They nodded.

Right, how could you not, if you go to Loyola. I've seen a hundred pictures of them, but not the actual thing until now.

Felix said, Is that the stuff they call the boom boom sauce?

Sounds about right, Momo said. It's got a bunch of names and a bunch of hype and a bunch of side effects that people don't really understand. Some of that stuff that happened earlier this season with the football guys, apparently that was a scare tactic or something. They put out all these fake side effects to discourage athletes from trying them.

I think that's partly true, Tyson said. My brother is on the football team, so he gives me some of the inside scoop. Regardless, it doesn't explain why this big guy is bringing them around in his pocket and tossing them all over the poker table. All the people I know, Kirby you'd be the last person I'd expect to be packing these pretty.

At that they gave Kirby the floor. He told him about how he ran Paul down outside the dance and then literally stumbled into two of the football guys and Bryce.

It happened so quickly, he said. Bryce must have been portioning them out as they were walking, and when we tripped into each other, some must have fallen into my jacket when they spilled. I'm not surprised. Those pockets were big as baseball mitts. I found them the next day when I was cleaning out my pockets, and I've been sort of mulling over what to do with them ever since. Then I made the connection. The real point I'm getting at is this though: Paul's got these. Not a few either. I mean like dozens and dozens. I walked away and that's when I heard Bryce call out to Paul to help clean his stash up. Meaning Paul's stash..

All right, so who's taking the first one, Momo cracked. See if they're all they're hyped up to be? He took one and tossed it in the air and threw it back.

Oh shut up Momo, Kirby said.

I'm just joking, geez ..

I know you are, but I'm seriously worried about Paul.

Yeah, since when?

Since now, since recently, since he hasn't been acting himself. Even though we've never been best buddies, I hate to see him like that and he's my teammate, so...

So Paul's sinking, is that what you're saying Kirby? Tits said.

Yeah, that's what I'm saying. He's in a trance. A dark trance. We need to snap him out of it, give him a shock to his system.

Before he goes over the edge?

He might be over the edge already.

Tits brought his envelope out. He peeled it open with his finger and set the two papers inside side by side.

He said, Go ahead, take one and pass it around. The content speaks for itself.

The garage turned quiet as they read the two sheets, and a dread feeling filled their guts. Between the pills and the papers, they came to an understanding among themselves, then they departed.

Plan of attack

They set up a three pronged attack. A way to bring Paul down successively by piercing the armor of his pride. They decided to keep Coach Brennan out of it for as long as possible, and see how Paul responded to the material Tits had and the pills Kirby had confiscated. After the poker night, they told Sam and Dave what they had found out and what they were planning. Those two, it turned out, had been planning their own scheme for bringing Paul down.

After practice at the end of the week, the team minus Paul convened to square their plan of attack. Dave explained how earlier that night, on homecoming, he had a similar experience to Kirby's with Paul.

He said, I went up to him between songs and asked how he was and he cussed me out and said a bunch of sick stuff about my girlfriend, who was standing behind me. I had to apologize to her afterward. But she said something that stayed with me. She said, Don't worry about it. That's not Paul talking. That's whatever he's hooked on. We both assumed it was just alcohol, that is until Kirby's side of the story. Sam and I also had a weird experience with him on the back of the bus a few weeks back. He was saying all kinds of stuff. Jumbling sentences, missing words. We let it go, but I'm with you guys that it's now or never.

Sam pulled out his phone. I've been holding on to this for a while now, not sure what to do with it.

The team huddled around his screen and he pressed play. It was a shaky, but clean video of Paul's hazing Kirby the night of the retreat. With a few months' perspective on it, the video appeared that much more appalling, raunchy, and aggressive than they remembered.

I'm surprised you took that, Momo said.

I'm surprised I took it too. You partly inspired it, actually. It was after you got your dog bite, and I felt like Paul was way off. I needed to put some guardrails up, but I also didn't want to get up in his face. So when the hazing started, he saw me take out the phone and got upset, and I told him I was capturing team memories we'd look back on and laugh at. Hoping that was actually the case, instead of what it turned out to be. Right now he's like a semi without brakes heading downhill, and all of us need to jump in front to stop it.

You think he's been using that stuff since then? The glit?

I doubt he was using it then, but shortly after, when he started hearing about what it could do, how it's supposed to calm you down instantly, give you on demand runners high, rinse out your system quickly, and wipe your short-term memory. I wouldn't be surprised.

Wipes your short-term memory? Tits said. And that's supposed to be a selling point?

Yeah, think about it. You're about to do something you know is wrong, and your conscience, if it's still operating, is giving you hell. And remember, it's Paul right? Top of the food chain, top athlete, popular, everybody loves him. All the honor stuff, awards. So the stakes are high. His conscience must be screaming and screaming not to do it. But then you pop one of these things and the screaming goes away, the guilt disappears, all those thoughts flying at you go away. Your body still performs at its peak, and as it pisses out of your system it leaves a big white street down the middle of your memory. Meaning all that guilt, all that reservation, and conscience gagging you felt just before, feels fuzzy, feels imaginary, like it didn't even happen. That's why it's so addictive. That's why it's so deadly. You never feel the pain. When you drink, you feel the hurt the next day. But with this stuff it's just a blur. Now, I'm no expert. That's just what I've heard. Paul could have been taking it and taking it, and every day he's taking it it still feels like day one. But what I fear is that it might progress until his conscience is like that beat up stop sign on the exit to the high school. Tipped over, bent in half, graffitied. Can't even tell it's a stop sign. Everybody rolls up and rolls past. It works that way for a time. But then someone comes the other way. In this case, this speed demon, he nudged Felix. Tears the old records like they're confetti. Then there's a crash and it's going to be ugly.

Stage one

Stage one: break the trance. Get him angry. Tick him off. Excite his rage. Create a diversion and find the stash, then slip the first letter in and let him sit with it.

The meet before counties was Lakeland, and that's what they did. The bus ride was quiet. The team was like a stealth squad ready to spring into action. No one said anything about Paul's eyes, but it was just as Kirby described. They looked lizard skinned. Saggy and fiery red around the rims. Nothing that makeup could cover up entirely. While the race was underway Momo went searching for the stash. He opened Paul's bags at the team tent. He dug through all the pockets but found nothing at first.

Nothing in the wallet, nothing in the phone case, nothing in the traveler's size first aid kit. Nothing in the duffle bag but socks and shirts.

Meanwhile time flew. The race went like clockwork. Felix scorched the field again. He did it with his same quicksilver stride and easy-going cadence. Paul, hard as he tried, hard as he pushed, came in a distant second.

Momo had to hurry. The one clue that kept him going when he was tempted to give up was a small tube of skin tone foundation which Paul had likely applied to his eyes. Momo rummaged frantically. Many of the team by then had come in and were doing their best to detain Paul at the finish line. Until they got some sign for Momo he found something. He was ready to give up. It felt like a left down, like maybe all their speculation was just that, speculation and nothing more. The fabricated result of groupthink.

Then, as he was stuffing everything back, something caught his eye. It was a blue pack of gum from the same compartment as the wallet and the phone in the keys. He had rummaged past it before. This time he picked it up and looked at it closer. It struck him as odd. At first he didn't know why, but then it was obvious. He never remembered Paul chewing gum before. But there was something else too. The pack wouldn't close properly. When he opened it, he noticed that the front row of silver wrapped sticks stuck up a tad too high, preventing the flap from closing around them. He took one of the sticks out. Then two. That's when his eyes lit up. Bingo!

Buried under the row of gum were a dozen small glittery pills. He snapped a picture for evidence, put all the stuff back, then placed the first envelope in the front of Paul's backpack where he would find it later.

He gave the team a thumbs up.

Stage one: check.

That night the runaway semi took its first massive swerve. Paul found the envelope as he was taking out his books. It was sealed and unaddressed. Wondering what it was, he tore it open and right away the writing jumped out at him. It was Presses' hand. His eyes skimmed the text and he saw his name, and he knew it was about him. It was dated the week before the team got the news that Press was gone. From the top he read…

To my replacement, a few notes about Paul, the kid I call Slobbers. Most of the kids are simple. They're fast or they're not. They've got it or they don't. They try or they don't. Paul's less simple. Top runner. Hard worker. Hard on himself. Seeks to please... gorgeous athlete, really fine, except when it's close. If he's ahead the whole race, he stays ahead and sweeps the competition clear. But if somebody so much as stays at his heels, passes him, or gains on him (you won't see it much) - you can see the fear come over his face. He folds, gets self conscious. The race moves from the ground to his head. And he never wins the latter. He loses heart. His legs do stupid things. His feet flop like fish. It's like he forgets his own basic stride. I've seen it in other guys like him, with BIG TALENT. They're plenty of them out there and they all think they're 'the one'.

Even if he ekes out the win, or loses by a hair and looks like he's gnashing his teeth in the agony of his effort, it's a show. Some mental vaudeville to hide the stupendous collapse. To hide the fact he threw in the towel a mile back when someone started competing. He likes winning, he doesn't like competing. They all do. I know his breed. I've seen many record breakers pass through the doors and go on to be average insurance salesmen.

Paul, being a BIG TALENT, doesn't like anything close. Resents it. Any race of consequence in which his pure talent might be tested. He works hard too. Sure. But he works hard to protect his talent. We've talked this through before. If it gets through, time will tell. Lot of guys nod their heads and keep doing what they've always done.

His dad's no help. His dad ran d1, heaped with god given speed like his son. I've had a couple throwdowns with this guy. Freshman year I said you're crippling your kid telling him he's a talent. I'm not trying to contradict you, but he doesn't need to focus on being talented. It creates a dilemma every time he's got to work for it.

Really work for it. I've told Paul, what happens if some kid from a school in the country with no program and half your precious talent whips you to shreds and shits all over your talent, because he just plainly smoked it at the end? Gassed it all the way home and didn't give a damn when he was passing you about how talented you are and he's not because you're just two muddy sets of legs clawing at each other for the finish.

How bout that? For the kid from the country school, it's just a good race, an amazing performance. And he moves on, keeps training, keeps running, trying to claw regardless if he stones another goliath or not. He keeps running. But the other has a meltdown. He withdraws himself, writes off practice, rejects the sport, gets stuck in gloomy moods where he becomes fatalistic, self-doubting, bitter toward the talent that let him down or his coach or whatever. It's a real crisis. And crises are important because people, whether they like it or not, are pliable, and I try to bend them back the right way.

Have I done enough with Paul? I doubt it. Sadly. I know him. I like the kid. I really like the kid. But he worries me. He's got a lot going for him. Maybe too much. There'll come a day when he'll come to you with his tail between his legs and don't sugar it up. Say he beat your ass because he ran like hell and you didn't. He worked his ass off and you didn't. Tell him we got training to do.

Everyone of his kind I've given the same spiel. And every time they hear it, they think I'm punishing them. They think I'm downgrading them by not mentioning that tired refrain of talent. I'm not. I'm rewarding the kid, if he ever wises up. The best reward you can give someone who whimpers out like that is to say cut the bullshit and hit the track. Don't pity yourself and go hide and stare at your belly button, wondering what it all means. Hit the track. Hit the hills. Dig in. Cry uncle. Cry uncle a few more times. And then after a week of existential meltdown and rumors behind my back about how I'm treating kids like garbage and a horrible coach - they come back, and start running the miles again. It's like a dose of medicine. It's like getting over the flu.

Slobbers. He's good, not the best, but very good, yes. Goes as far as hard work takes him. Loves his own myth a bit too much. One day will pay for it, I'm sure...

Paul read it twice over. The second time the paper trembled in his hands. When he finished he felt weak. He stared at the letter long enough that the words seemed to peel off the page like demon animations, capering around him, taunting him in Bill Presses ragged voice. Phrases sliced at him like razors.

He's good, not the best...

Have I done enough with Paul? I doubt it...

They're plenty of them out there and they all think they're 'the one'.

For Paul it was like staring into a crystal ball. Reading a horoscope. Or worse, an obituary. A part of him died. It was one thing to believe himself to be the runner he thought he was. A god of running, a chosen one, a specimen picked out by Bill Press to be a legend. It was another thing for a few blunt words on a page to change all that. To flip it upside down. To take a swinging sledgehammer to his porcelain self image.

Bucket list punch

The letter was a move designed to bring Paul to submission. Paul assumed it was the work of one of the underclassmen. One of those he had clashed with all season. His first thought was Momo. He had seen Momo messing around with the bags at the meet. He texted him that night a picture of the opened envelope.

Did you send this? he wrote.

He got no reply, which he took as affirmative.

The next day, Paul came back elastic, pretended he had shrugged off the whole thing. He smiled and was upbeat and mentioned nothing to anyone at practice about the letter. But the day after he was back to his old self. The thought of someone else having that letter and reading it before him infuriated him.

He confronted Momo after lunch. He pulled him into the hall.

Why'd you do it?

Do what?

Don't play dumb with me. I know you did it. Paul tried to talk calmly. He had a toothpick he played between his teeth and left hanging off the side of his lips.

You spend all season being a dirty Mexican, faking a dog

bite and lying through your teeth.

As he talked he stepped closer and closer till he was a foot for Momo's face.

Paul never got a chance to finish his abuse. Momo nailed him in the face, so hard that Paul chipped one of his front teeth and swallowed it.

You think that's something? Momo said, There's more where that came from. A lot more, esse. That's not even half of what you deserve.

Momo recapped the episode for the other guys later that day. With a shake of his head, he kissed his knuckles. He said, I'm not going to say I liked it, or that I enjoyed it, or that it was the sportsman thing to do. …But I kind of liked it. And he deserved it. Dude was up in my grill saying all kinds of stuff. I'm glad I could check that one off my bucket list.

What was on your bucket list? someone asked.

I've always wanted to punch someone as hard as I could right in the face.

So is that the real reason you hit him? Kirby joked.

No, but that's why they call it hitting two birds with one stone.

The situation was getting ugly, but it was working. Paul was breaking. Or so they thought.

The video

They followed the first cut with the second. They released the video of Paul's drunken haze on the team retreat. It landed like a stone in water, the waves rippling outward and reaching unprecedented publicity.

Mike Nichols saw the video first. Then his staff, including Coach Brennan. Then the principal and vice principals of the high school. Sam knew, the whole team knew, that releasing the footage put the whole team in jeopardy. It would expose them to any form of punishment the school saw fit. Still, they agreed to proceed.

The school suspended the team from all competition for a week. During that time the administration formed a clearer picture of the situation. One by one, over many days, the players held interviews with the principal, Mike Nichols, student counselors and the school's mental health professional.

The upshot of the interrogation was that the team at large was warned, but exonerated. Paul was held exclusively responsible for the abuse documented through the video and subsequent investigation. He was stripped of the high school career athletic award he had received earlier that year. He was required to meet with the school's mental health professional once a week from there until graduation. He was disqualified from all competition for the rest of the season. And he was required to make a satisfactory apology to the team and coach by the end of the season. He could practice if he wanted, participate in team spirit if he wanted, but his season was effectively terminated.

When the rest of the school heard the news, the students and the staff were shocked. Additionally, the original video leaked beyond the walls of Loyola High. Some of the students at rival schools created funny spoofs of Paul on top of the rock pile, transposing animated heads of Bugs Bunny, Captain America, Captain Morgan, and even Bill Press over Paul's. His spotless name was scrapped from the ballot list for best all around.

What effect did all of this have on Paul? From the outside, it looked like little or none. His old elastic ability came out again. He denied nothing, avoided no one, not even his team who had taken arms against him he knew. In the best way he could, he stripped the drama and sensation down to size by calling all of it just the dumb mistake. Making it seem as though they were nothing but guys being guys. In short, in the face of damaging evidence, Paul continued to uphold and defend the only image he had of himself.

He played off his terminal season with more PR about it being an opportunity to show moral support. Under all appearances, Paul may have been swerving for his life. He may have felt the noose around his neck and the water boiling, but he kept taking it and taking it, brushing it off and brushing it off, smiling and taking it as if it were no big deal. He was a 10-ton gorilla that would not go down, no matter how many shots were fired at it. In the meantime he kept hanging out with another ten ton gorilla named Bryce Cooley.

Bryce Cooley

Whether people say so or not, they like a prick star athlete. They like someone with great abilities and great liabilities. Someone who swaggers and puffs, but also crashes and burns magnificently. People want a bit of hero worship with a bit of disdain. Someone to revere and someone to drag down to their own level of mediocrity.

That year, when Paul's glorious season began to implode, he renewed his friendship with one of those guys. A stud named Bryce Cooley. Bryce was the star receiver on the football team, a kid blessed with height, frame, agility, good looks, a dad who was a millionaire, and a mom who had once been Miss Illinois, and now looked with all her nips and tucks to be about only 10 years older than her son.

All football season long, Bryce wore loose cut off shirts that showed his stacked muscles underneath. He was a towhead, his hair buzzed on the sides with a long careless swoop on top. He had a big, gregarious smile and mild acne on his shoulders, and everywhere he went he carried a shaker protein bottle with a red lid and a huge set of black headphones which he hung on the straps of his backpack.

The trouble with Bryce Cooley is that he was a known abuser of the bottle, and famously, (infamously), got in hot water. Two years in a row, on the same night he helped win the state championship for his team, he got in a near fatal car crash. The first time his teammate died. The next time he was spared again but his teammate lost an arm which was severed between the car and the tree it ran into.

Both times the real story was covered up by the athletic director who was good friends with his father. That year Press quit, there was no car crash yet, but he started smuggling glit into the locker room. Bryce described the new performance enhancing pill as *Adderall, Xanax, Creatine and sex all mixed together and clean as a spring. It goes right through your system without a hitch.*

A few guys on the football team knew about it, but not many.

When Paul was knocked off his high horse, he turned to Bryce for refuge. Paul denied any shady dealing with Bryce, but the other guy's knew Bryce's track record. The kid never made one splash, always two, and often three or four. Though Paul insisted he wouldn't have anything to do with that, the others doubted him. They saw them spending more time together, chewing the fat after class or after practice.

The power of Bryce was that he evinced a sort of high blown machismo, that even when it blew up in flames, was still somewhat revered and respected. He had that party starting mentality, that big drive, that barnstorming personality that crashed through feebleness, that had a reckless lust for adventure, a freewheeling state of mind to seize the day and have his fun now, during college and high school, before settling into a career of eminent respectability like his father.

He was intent on doing his knuckleheading now, and to do it well, and as full tilt as he could get it. He was also a flatterer and a showy personality, who often shouted out in class at the great way the teacher was doing their teaching. Disingenuous? Sure. But also effective. And in doing so he molded around himself a protective layer of likability. When some of his misdemeanors came to light, the harshness was diffused by the layer of likability.

He had free reign in a way, and he used high school like a jungle gym.

Toward the end of the season Bryce became for Paul a surrogate for Press. Offering him the foul mouth and the hard-boiled gridiron wisdom that he could not get from Coach Cal or from his team.

Bethany Clayton

There was a third bullet, a silver bullet for the gorilla that the team did not want to use right away. They waited to see what would happen. If Paul would eventually come forward and make a statement to the rest of them, or if he would smile off the rest of the season, covering his tracks with fatuous apologies.

Then something happened they didn't expect. A week after the video made news, Bethany Clayton came forward and told her story about Paul. What he said to her the night he asked her to homecoming and she turned him down. She claimed he told her he was going to take her to the dance and that he would not take no for an answer. At first she thought he was playing. She told him she was going with someone else, and he asked who and she told him. Then he said the first thing that frightened her. He said, referring to her date, *if he's still around*. He said it like a nasty joke. He told her she needed to call it off with that guy and that she'd be glad she did if she went with Paul. She was feeling extremely uncomfortable then. But Paul continued to 'press'. That's the word she used multiple times to describe his way of trying to intimidate her to change her mind. When she told him no a final time, she said Paul laughed and said, *It wouldn't matter anyway because grinders find a way, and I'm going to make you mine, dead or alive, with your consent or without.*

Chilling words. It was these chilling words that began to bring the house down. Paul, who had skated past his earlier allegations by downplaying them, tried to deny them outright here. But that proved the fatal tactic. For one, Bethany Clayton was a trustworthy source. Her team and all her friends believed her without a doubt, from the moment she came forward. Secondly, Paul had overused his swagger.

Nothing of the sort happened, he said. I would never say anything like that, and I never did.

The campaign of utter denial was an utter failure. No matter how much he denied it, the nastiness of the words and the suggestion they created clung to him like smoke on fire. No longer did he waltz down the hall with his shoulders thrown back and his smile beaming. He hid for cover in his band of football hooligans. But not even them, not even Bryce with his winning personality, could win this one for Paul.

The more Paul denied it, the more it served to strengthen the case against him. The fire had already started. The Bethany story was lighter fluid.

Paul was falling through fiery hoops. His reputation was in freefall. It seemed like it could get no worse for him.

But then it got worse.

The call

Paul showed up in the locker room one afternoon after practice. He had missed practice to have his one hour a week session with the school mental health professional. Coach Cal was giving a pep talk to the rest of the guys. Paul was dressed in his street clothes and carried in his eyes a look of terrifying anger. He sat down smoldering, unwilling to look any of them in the eye. Near the end of Cal's remarks, Paul's phone went off. It was a flashback to the first day they met Coach Cal and Paul, taking another call, rose to leave.

This time though, when he checked his phone his face went white. The whole team noticed it. Without a word he just got up and went.

When he had left, Coach Cal said, What I'm about to say doesn't leave this room. But at this point, with all that's been going on, I feel obligated to tell you what I think that call is about. And the only reason I know is because I got my own call this afternoon, preparing me for it.

The team sat on the edge of their seats, wondering what he was going to say.

Paul lost his scholarship to Oregon. The coach over there has been keeping tabs on all the stuff going on here. That's the short of it. I'm not here to air dirty news for the hell of it. I don't know Paul as well as you guys do, but I'm sharing it with you to prepare you. It might get worse before it gets better.

Kick the dog

The news rocked all of them, not just Paul. It especially rocked Sam and Dave, who had been with him, ran with him, battled with him all those years.

The team had a moment of recollection following the update. Is this what they wanted when they set their plan in motion? Had they gone too far? Had they overreached in their attempt to pull Paul loose of the hell he was creating? Had they sabotaged him?

After contemplating the matter, they determined they had not gone far enough.

The surgery was incomplete. The knife had not gone deep enough. It was time for the final plunge.

Sam and Paul

It was strange to think of Tits, of all people, holding the ace up his sleeve. An ace that cut deeper than the others and that brought the whole blighted year full circle.

It was another piece of paper. Not quite a letter. The team folded it in thirds and packed it in a standard envelope. They had all read it. It was hard to read. They debated giving it to him now, when the wound of his lost scholarship was still fresh, and they decided yes, give it to him now: kick the dog when he was down.

This time Sam stepped up. He wanted to deliver the message in person. At the start of the season, he considered Paul one of his best friends. Now, he was just shy of an enemy. Dave offered to come too, but Sam said, That's all right. If you find me dead in a ditch somewhere you know what happened.

A dark joke, but only slightly a joke.

For a day after the scholarship news, Sam called Paul and texted him a dozen times and got no response. He decided the only thing to do at that point was to go to his house and confront him head on.

He came to the front door and knocked. The house was dark inside. Paul's mother came to the front door. When she saw who it was she did not open the door all the way. She left it cracked, and she spoke through the crack.

Yes? she said, with a suspicious question in her voice. Sam had known her for as long as he had known Paul. She had always been kind to him, but that afternoon she looked as though she had never seen him before, like he was a stranger.

Is Paul home?

Her head turned inside, upstairs, as if she were unsure of the answer or unwilling to give it.

What's it about?

I wanted to check on Paul. See how he's doing.

She kept her hand on the knob as he spoke. She looked inside again. Her expression wavered. She said, Todays' probably not a good day to drop by. He's been feeling under the weather lately.

(Yeah, that's one way to put it, Sam thought.)

Wait here, she said. She slipped inside and he watched her through the glass door as she made her way up the staircase behind her, slowly, quietly, tip-toeing up the steps as if there were a baby in the house sleeping which she was afraid of waking.

As she was going up, something else caught Sam's attention though. He heard a door close. Not loud, and not from upstairs, but from the back of the house.

Sam had been to that house so many times he knew the sounds it made. For some reason, he felt like he was being deceived. He quickly hopped off the front porchway and jogged along the side of the house to a waist high chain link gate and opened the latch to the backyard.

As soon as he rounded the corner he saw Paul on the far end of the yard, about to leave, sneaking away.

The figure he saw did not look like the Paul Stafford he had always known. It reminded him of a white trash punk kid. Paul wore a red cut off shirt, the same style Bryce Cooley often wore, with a big Georgia bulldog on the front. He wore a pair of black baggy basketball shorts that ended halfway down his shins. Adidas slippers and Nike tube socks.

Paul stopped, his back facing Sam. Sam called his name. Paul flipped the sunglasses that were sitting on his forehead down over his eyes, a move that immediately struck Sam as defensive, as wary.

It's just me, Paul. Where are you going?

Paul hesitated like his mother. His hand reached for the latch but did not lift it. When Sam came closer, Paul remained in place, tense, like a rabbit ready to make a run for it.

I'm not going anywhere, Paul said. He lowered the latch, but stayed where he was.

Sam thought about calling his obvious bluff, but there was no time for pointless bickering.

What are you doing here, showing up unannounced, asking stupid questions like where are you going? Aren't you the one that knows the answer to that question better than anybody? Are you here to prove a point? You here to deliver another one of your messages? I can see you holding something in your hand. You know all the news, I'm sure. I'm not going anywhere, thanks to you. Not a damn place. You can go now. Finish up your stakeout, or whatever the hell you're doing. You're a traitor and you stabbed me in the back. Go and take all your secrets with you.

What are you talking about, secrets?

I don't want it, Paul hissed. I don't want to read whatever it is you're holding. I can smell it on you.

Paul, Sam pleaded, What are you talking about? I just want

to talk to you.

Oh, do you? And do you also want to secretly record your conversation with me so you can use it against me some time?

No, I only want to talk.

Prove it.

Sam took the envelope he was holding behind his back and tore it in half four times. He put the shreds in his pocket.

Sam couldn't read Paul's eyes behind his glasses, but he knew it surprised Paul, that he did that.

Now, can you take off your glasses, please?

What does that matter?

So I can feel like I'm talking to a real person.

Paul lifted them to his forehead, reluctantly. He took a second to lift his eyes enough to look Sam square. But when he did, Sam couldn't hide his reaction. He was appalled. Paul's eyes were gunked with mucus and eye discharge. They were brown and yellow spotted. Glazed with fear. The liver skinned eyes of a kicked dog.

The sun shot over the roof of the house and hit him where he stood like a spotlight, inflaming his sickly appearance and vacant stare. He looked like someone who should be taken to the Infirmary. On top of that, when he lifted his lips, Sam could see his chipped tooth, where Momo had punched him as hard as he could. He looked absolutely terrible.

What have you been doing? Sam asked.

Paul shrugged, frowned his mouth.

Figuring out my life. What little I have left, he said in his dejected voice.

Sam stared at the desperate, despicable thing standing apart from him. He was unsure what to say, if anything. Sam had come to learn in moments like that, that even at that tender age, with all their lives before them, tragedies abound in life. And one of those tragedies was that despair could so waste a figure to its bones. He had come to see that one. He had come to see that part of life was sockfull of pettiness and fickleness, of bitter soulscalding slavery to one idle or another. That fear, suspicion, jealousy, could grind a man until he was less than a man.

Well, are you going to say something, or are you just going to look at me? Paul said. He said it heartless, like he was awaiting some judgment over his pissedoff, snakepit life. Someone to tell him what he knew already.

He had reached a point of no disguise. A place where the smile of success and the camouflage of accomplishment and the angry smear of war paint ran off his face like clown's make up. He was there, all of him. Small, plain, miserable..

No, I don't have much to say to you, Paul. I only wish that something or someone would release you from the fear you're living in. You look whipped, gun shy. I can barely recognize you. You look starved and beaten, like some POW. And that's your choice. You look worse than Momo's dog bite. And I'll tell you on behalf of all the other guys, you've made the whole year a dog bite. A big unhealed wound that keeps getting infected. Don't you see that, Paul? No bullshit. No more bullshit. All year long you've been trying to channel Press. Your face has been red as a beat and splotched, and your eyes look like that. And you go around in yelling fits half the time. And the other half you're in a daze and no one knows where Paul is. You became an impostor. No one knows where the real Paul went. The only reason we came at you is to pull you out of this ditch you've been digging. It wasn't me alone, so don't call me a traitor. It was all of us. Worried to death about you. I hope you'll understand that. If not today, then one day eventually. Enough, Paul, Enough, he said, with real feeling and emotion in his voice.

He sounded like he might break down and cry.

It's you, Paul. It's you. We need you. We don't need Press back. We need you. Get back to basics. Get back to running, Get back to all the stuff you love before you felt you had to prove anything to anyone. Get back to freshman year. Remember that? You and me and Dave, trying to do Mustache Mondays with the big boys. Except we couldn't grow mustaches, so we drew them on with sharpies. Remember when Press would say, I'm no philosophizer, I'm just a grump with a whistle and a stopwatch and a beer belly and a bark like a sawed-off shotgun?

That was like our third day of practice and we were like, oh shit.

Remember how he'd pull you aside sometimes and say, I know *you,* in that gravelly, sultry tone, crook his eye up at you and say it like he's picked you out of a hundred and set you on his private mantel with plans to groom you into the next King of Running...

Or how he'd say, Running won't get you off the hook or make you rich. If you want to make money with your bodies, go play football or be a prostitute? Don't run to get your shit together, don't run because you want to feel some Chariots of fire fairy dust. Run because you want to kick your own shit in the teeth, you want to kill your slews of excuses, you want to remember that horrible, horrible wrench in the stomach when you come to the line, when you hit that wall, when your body says NO, when some rival kid out kicks you in the last 100 yards. The muddy hills and the freezing downpours. You must know something more than pleasure then. What that something is remains a mystery, not a set of words. It's like asking you to describe the color red. And my duty lies in passing it on. Do you remember him saying any of that?

Remember how he'd say, You remind me of myself, all of you. Young, hot headed, full of bright ideas and big desires and big dreams. Good, bring it all, and be willing to scrap it all too. Remember how he said he had a coach back when he ran named Hicks. Who he hated and he said he swore he'd never be like. He'd never be a hard ass, washed up high school coach in a podunk city, just like he said he'd never cheat on his wife or spank his kids.

Sam had worked himself up with such feeling and emotion, Paul had never seen him like that before. He was moved by it. It struck a chord below the surface of his pain.

Why are you telling me all this, Sam?

Sam shrugged. So you don't forget. I would hate for you to do something that would make you forget what it's all been about, brother.

Yeah, well it's too bad they pulled the cord on him.

Sam shook his head. Paul, he said, he pulled it on himself… can't you see that?

Why are you really here? To take me down memory lane?

To talk to you.

I don't wanna talk.

Clearly, but you don't have to dodge everything I say, Paul. It's me. I'm not out to get you.

Oh really?

Yes, really.

Well you cost me my career…

Paul narrowed his sickly eyes on Sam.

You got to get over him, Paul. It's time.

Over who? Felix. Forget Felix. You think I care he took Sadie to…

Not Sadie. Her dad. I understand why you look up to him, Paul, I really do. We all did, in our own way. I wasn't just blowing smoke up your ass reminding you of all those things. His training helped you get records, championships, a scholarship to Oregon…but,

But what? What are you saying?

Just because you got those things doesn't mean you can keep them.

You son of a bitch. If my mom wasn't here…

Paul…I didn't mean to…

Yeah, well you did.

What was the point of you coming over here anyway, to have some intervention, tell the guys Paul's lost his mind and fucked his whole life over for nothing…

Is that what you think, Paul?

Pretty much.

I promise you you're wrong.

Really?! Is that why you plant that letter in my bag, convince Bethany to say what she said, and …

Paul, whatever's done is done. My biggest regret is not talking to you sooner, face to face. Like we are now. I kept thinking you were playing some game, or just letting your jealousy get the best of you, and you would snap out of it. But you kept digging and digging, and I'm sorry. I really am. I remember you told us once, every race was a second chance to outdo ourselves. But you don't believe in second chances, do you? You say you do, but you don't. You say all the right things. But you really don't want someone to get better than you. When it threatens you, all your virtues turn to smoke. You're a weasel like the rest of us.

Sam dug the scraps of torn paper out of his pocket and came up to Paul and shoved the contents in his hand.

Put the pieces together, he said. Then find another way.

Last message

Paul went away that afternoon and wandered. He went somewhere and did something and told no one. He was alone. He wanted to be alone. He wanted to hide in his thoughts, hide behind his glasses, but Sam's visit assaulted him. All the old memories came roaring back, all the things Sam remembered and shared began to occupy his thoughts, and he could see it all and hear it all again clearly, as if he were there freshman year, standing at his very first starting line, his legs shaking.

It struck him to the core.

He came home and sat on his bed and outturned the tatters of pages from his pockets. He began to fit them together, like a large jigsaw.

The first page was a piece of copy paper with three starts and stops of paragraphs on it. The first read,

To whom it may concern,

After 25 seasons of coaching, unfortunately I must resign due to unfortunate personal circumstances, of a nature...

It cut off.

The next began...

Dear Loyola Staff and Faculty,

After long consideration, I have decided to resign as head coach of the men's cross country team. The circumstances of my immediate departure are due to a relationship with a youn...

Here too the message cut off. But it was clear with each iteration Press was getting closer to the real truth of the matter.

At the end of the second message, Paul's mind began to finish the last message. A relationship with who, he thought? 'Young', was obviously the last word...

Young what? Teacher? He thought. The thought paralyzed him. His mind began to spin with who that might be. Which young teacher at Loyola did he have an affair with?

There was a fist in his throat, from anticipation now more than anything else. He kept reading.

The third false start note read...

Dear staff and whoever it may concern,

I'm resigning my post as men's cross country coach, as well as all teaching assignments, effective immediately... To my grave disappointment/dishonor, I have become intimately involved with a... The last line was scratched out and rewritten with a sanitary phrase, 'due to urgent personal matters I have decided...'

But the flip side of the page is where it all came out. The message was not typed, but handwritten. It ran from top to bottom, with tiny, tense pockets of notes in the margins. It was addressed to himself and apparently was written with no intent of being shared with anyone else. It was stripped of all the professional salutation and tone. It was written to himself.

It read...

Dear Bill,

Quit while you can... I will no longer be coaching the men's cross country team. I'm quitting. I've dug the pit deep enough. Now I must sit in it. Tell me Bill, what you've done, you sorry excuse of a coach and man.

Tell me it's true you've slept with two students, two young girls, seniors at the time you put these foul words down. One was a cheerleader at our school. The other a cheerleader at Nolensville. LD and RS. Their parents, faculty, coaches all know something, but not all. LD is pregnant. RS... don't know. Sheila knows all and the divorce is forthcoming. Sadie knows something. Every time I try to put down a message tendering my resignation, I feel like dying, like death. LD is pregnant, and going to keep the kid.

As I write this my hand is trembling and my mouth tastes like a sewer. I am 63 years old. I've spent the better part of my career telling the guys I coach their peckers will get them in more trouble than their mouths will. If they're not careful. And here I go, running off the deep end at the start of what may have been my finest season yet. You can build a life of some reputation over 20 years and have it all come crashing down overnight.

That's what I've done. And I will not go out during the light of day, but like a thief in the night, to my shame and dishonor and to the total disgrace of the program I helped establish. And I will not tell a word of my sins to my runners, for fear it will harm them in ways I cannot imagine at the time of my readiness.

That is the greatest hurt by far. Not to be willing, not to be able to tell them the truth, and hope that all this hell blows over.

I have not saved a dime to pay for the child to be born, though I imagine LD will steer the child as far away from me as possible, and she would be wise to.

Then down the page when the words 'foul and disgrace', one after another, line by line, an unbroken chain all the way down to the gutter, in all sizes and shapes of letters, done the way a kid does when they're practicing their signature.

Paul's eyes were wide open. The window to his bedroom was open too and the breeze hurried in and pushed back the curtains which made a soft click when they flapped against the wall.

Paul read the note again, wondering the next time if it was fabricated, if someone on the team had made it up in some elaborate way. But the more he read the more he realized none of them could have written a letter like that. He could hear Press in every line, could follow the letters as they became more wobbly and unneat, as they traveled down the page, and the hand found it harder and harder to write, to come to terms with the content of what he had written.

Paul's mother appeared in the doorway. She asked if he was all right and what Sam wanted, and if he needed anything.

He said, Can you leave me alone, that's all.

In the corner of the jigsaw page he saw a small scribble nearly lost in the gap where the pages came together. *Lauren Duffy*. That must have been the girl from Nolensville. Press had only used her initials in the actual message.

Paul typed her name into his phone and a picture of a girl taking a selfie with a baby bump and mid drift shirt and pink truck her hat came up on her social media feed. The text below the picture read, *Just a couple months before I meet my little buddy*.

He scrolled through all her pictures, and noticed that in the more recent pictures her hair was shorter and darker. Once a dirty blonde, she now had a raven black bob, with a streak of purple in it.

He clicked the phone off and sat forward on the edge of his bed, like he was looking down into a well. A dark image filled his mind and he could see it so vividly and so intensely his strained eyes hurt.

He shut them and rubbed them till they were red. Then he shook the vision off and got up. He went around the room stiff necked, looking for something. He opened his closet and found the shoe box under a pile of dirty clothes. He opened it, and using the tip of his thumbnail, cut the plastic wrapped sleeve of a dozen gum packets and began popping the pills out, scraping them into a small plastic baggie.

When the baggie was full, he zipped it up and zipped another one over it. He went downstairs and asked his mother if they had a meat tenderizer. She found the mallet looking tool from the drawer, and asked what he needed it for, and he said, Nothing.

He took it upstairs and pounded the pills on the window sill on top of a folded night shirt to muffle the sound.

When the pills were dust and glitter, he wiped the tenderizer clean and brought it downstairs. His mother said, Did it help? And he said, Yes. Then he went up and put the powder in the front pocket of his backpack. On his desk he had a printed calendar of the cross country season. Every race up till then had an X through it. But the very last race he circled three times.

County championships.

The very next day.

Pep talk

Dogs can feel a storm coming and men can too. They can sense bad news coming around the corner.

There was something off that day, something they could feel by collective intuition. The whole team was in a state of limbo. Ever since the Paul story made headlines, there was a question as to what would actually happen to the rest of the season. Would they compete? Would they not compete? Did they have enough runners to compete? Or would everything be drowned out by the incessant noise that began when shit hit the fan and all the news broke loose.

For a bunch of goofy kids who ordinarily got little or no fanfare, it was a peculiar place to be in. When they got off the bus they could feel the aura of attention and murmurs all around. People talking about them, talking about Paul, wondering if he would show up for this, his last high school race and support his team.

The rest of them had no idea. The best they knew was they were going to run as well as they could, given the circumstances and leave it at that.

Before the race, Coach Cal, in his talk to the team said, with a twinkle in his eye, Someone told me when I started this season there was going to be some drama. If they had told me it was going to be like this, I don't know if I would have signed up in the first place.

He laughed, but his tone was completely serious.

The best I can say at this point is, leave it all out there. Forget about results and focus on your run. Let it all hang out.

For that last race Momo suited up. Not by choice, by necessity. His long unhealed leg was still on the mend. When he pulled on his singlet and bib, it glared under the white sports tape he wrapped around it, along with his pale legs. The guys gave him a hard time for those pale legs, but they gave him pats on the back for going out and being willing to race.

A few moments before the race, the team gathered under the tent, watching the weather build overhead. All day it brooded. All day muscular cumulus clouds stacked across the sky, growing thick and ripe with rain. It was fitting weather to run in. It was dark then, and the cool air sent shivers up their legs and down their backs. They were quiet for a time, each of them speculating if the storm would come, and if so, what it signified. For it seemed to signify something. It seemed to come over them like a coda, like the definitive black lines at the end of a sheet of music. This was the end, the sky said.

Although Felix looked his usual cool self, inside he was nervous and jittery. It was the final hill. The bell at the top of the manor. He had broken four of Paul's once untouchable records in a span of only a few months. Now he was going for the 5th.

Kirby asked if anyone had seen the water cooler come and they said no. Tyson handed him his water bottle. Kirby drank some and spit it out. His eyes moved along the ground where they sat like he was thinking something through. Turning something over in his thoughts.

He was there waiting like a tall, deep voiced tree. Something beastly came over him. The sleeping dragon roused. He blushed to the roots of his hair and then his tender laugh withered. All day he thought about the shotgun season, the cesspool of drama, all the morale kicked over like a yard sign. Then he was done with it. He exhaled all the shitty news and stood there in the bullpen, swaying dangerously like a tree chainsawed down to its last jagged fibers, ready to crash at any point. Ready to channel it…

Then he stopped. He looked around and cleared his throat. The other guys looked up.

He said, In all my years running on this team, I never gave a pep talk. I always wanted to, so I guess I am here and now.

He put his hand on the back of a dark green folding chair in front of him. He paused, collecting his thoughts.

I feel like this year has been the best year and the worst year of my life. The worst is that we're staring at the end of the season. I'm going to miss these guys like hell, he nodded over to Sam and Dave. But at the same time, I feel like we've been choking all year, scared all year, distant with one another all year. And we all know why. But it doesn't change the fact.

Then this guy comes along and shatters about every good record in the book, and I feel like it's all just being passed over, ignored because of you know what. But that's the worst part. And from here on out it's dead to me, and it's dead to you too, if you're real stags. All that dies here on this race, on this course, on this day. Under these storm clouds, in these short shorts, against all these other goobers out there running against us. Forget about them. This is about us.

As his voice grew louder, he saw Paul join the back of the tent. He wasn't dressed to run, but at least he wasn't wearing his glasses, and he was wearing a stag shirt. Kirby continued.

Felix told me something earlier this season that stayed with me, that I feel like passing on now. I asked him once what he thought about when he ran, when he was tearing through the competition. And he said, he didn't think. He *hears*. I said, what does that mean, you hear a voice or something telling you to keep going or to pick it up?

Then he pulls out his boom box and plays this song. I'll never forget it. I forget what the song was, but something clicked when he did that. Right as he said that I had this phrase in my head which has been there ever since. *Run with a song in your head.* Run with the song in your head. I feel like that's not just a word for the track. It's a word for life. And I intend to run by it today.

No more arguing, fighting, pointing blame at anyone other than yourself…

There was a generous uptick in his voice, an encouraging sweetness.

If you argue today, argue with your weakness, your excuses for pulling up short. If you fight, fight your fear, fight the inertia in your legs and in your mind. Don't run to save yourself, run to give yourself. Get unhypnotized by defeat. And if you want to blame something…

Felix shouted out, BLAME IT ON THE JACKET!!

Tits shouted it too and the boys went wild at that. They cheered and Kirby flushed again and grabbed the back of the chair.

Hell yeah! he pumped, That's right! Blame it on the jacket! This is it, boys, he said, his voice cracking. This is the race.

This is the gauntlet. This is the sweet honey you've been checking out all year…

Whistles… Woo's… 'Ok Kara Klein' Tyson called out, as Kirby smirked and tried to stay focused on his pep talk.

No more looking over shoulders saying should've could've would've. Shit or get off the pot. There's a point where the only way to go faster is to go faster. There's a point where the girl's waiting for you to kiss her and you better kiss her or she'll walk out the front door. If you've been stuck, if you hit a wall, you break through only by breaking yourself. Give yourself the finger and say the hell with you legs, and the hell with you lungs on fire, and fainting spells, and legs heavy as hell. And you turn yourself inside out, you turn yourself to a terror, a ballyhoo, a stormcloud cruising with a load of lightning and you unload. There is no shortcut. You are the obstacle.

Today, channel what you've got. Channel your good, your bad, your ugly. Channel your first kiss, your last kiss, your mother's love, your father's fury, the skeleton in your closet, all of it. Use it all to put some sexy in your stride. Loser's weep and whine, but Grinders find a way! Grinders find a fuckin way!! Lets gooooo!!

He whipped the chair off the ground and flung it across the tent. Then he stripped off his jersey and flipped it inside out, from white to red. Red, the color of fire, the color of blood. The boys jumped to their feet, inspired, and did the same. All the white turned red. They stamped their feet and snorted like bulls. Someone dragged the water jug over and they drank and cheers'ed and bumped chests and then the whistle blew and they got quiet and it was time to race.

Counties

To say that the race was unforgettable was an understatement. To say that it was a race for the movies, for television, was closer to the truth, but still tame. If any medium of art could have captured the feeling of that race, it might have been a painting.by Van Gogh - the painting of the wheatfields on the cusp of the storm, the lone black bird riding the wind and the tall shocks of grain cowering under the heavy dark blue sky. It felt ominous and grand and sacred. Full of unspoken danger, if you can imagine a foot race being so.

Kirby had a strange feeling at the start line, as everybody took their mark. Time slowed. He glanced back and saw Paul standing behind them, looking on with his hands in his pockets. Then he glanced aside. Tyson and Tits were at his three o'clock. Silently, Tyson motioned to Tits. He raised his hand in the air, held it out in front of him, the fingers spread evenly. He nodded his head like he was trying to communicate something. His hand was perfectly still and steady. All three sets of eyes stared at the still hand. Kirby thought of Paul's hands in his pockets, then of Tyson's steady hand, and he felt some connection between the two but couldn't say it. He knew Tyson trembled before races. His hand got the shakes.

Sometimes he threw up. Both of those were good signs that he was primed to go.

Right as Tyson was whispering, Feel that? to Tits, the gun fired. They were off. The momentum from the first quarter mile wiped their minds blank. They ran. Ahead of them it rained suddenly. The curtain of cold precipitation fell like a guillotine which had been waiting over them all day. It battered the hills muddy and bathed the course in a murky yellow light. By the time they reached the first slick gulches, the rain had relented. It traveled down the course ahead of them, as though it had a mind for tracking them. For three quarters of a mile it did this. The rain fell and relented, fell and relented, tempting the runners into its toils. Then it stopped and stood. The pack ran into it. They were swallowed in the sodden roar.

And that was not the strangest part. Most of the stags began to feel a high coming over them. Later they would describe it as like a silky skin that grew over them, relaxing their bodies, darkening their eyes. Dave said he felt his tongue go numb. The sensation glazed their expressions and gave them a zombie-like dead reckoning for the finish line. It sheltered them from the onslaught of nerves, from the tremors of anxiety, from the fears and dreadedness of losing...

Then all at once it backfired.

As they crossed into the rain, Kirby saw Felix, who had broken away from the pack, begin to shake his arm wildly. Then his leg. Then all at once his body went rigid like a plant and he went down sideways and remained frozen on the turf. Before anyone could assess him Dave went down after him, then Tyson, then Sam: boom, boom, boom, one after another down the line like dominos, like dropped flies.

What the hell was going on? Whatever *it* was, was moving backward. Two other runners from other teams went down too. Then two more

Kirby was next in line, and right when he thought he'd catch it, the angel of death passed over him, and struck Tits, at his rear. The last thing he saw of Tits was his hands becoming gnarled like a witches, and his eyes rolling back in his head. A little gasp, then he crashed like a plank as well..

Any good, reasonable teammate, under those conditions, would have stopped and called the race off and sought help. It was no angel in their midst. It was a demon of discord weaving through the pack, mixing with some weird mass hysteria…

In two minutes, a quarter of the field was down; some rubbing their heads, some shaking out their legs. Most of the stags were still stiff as boards. They were far enough away from the officials and coaches that no one knew what was going on. But the most surprising thing of all is that Kirby kept going, and Momo too.

They were the only two from the team left in the race.

Rapido, rapido big boy!! Momo shouted after Kirby. Don't stop, don't look back. Rapido! Rapido!

Momo was limping along, but his words were like fire to the big kid. The dragon awoke. The rain and the wreckage had broken his rhythm but he regained it, wiped his face with arm and surged forward onto the broad path beaten to black mush.

Halfway through he had taken the lead. He had no idea. The thought never crossed his mind. What crossed his mind was a feeling like he was at war with something; at war with that demon of discord strewing his teammates behind him,

The dark sky gaped at him beyond and he went toward it,

toward that yellow murky light that looked like the end of the world. His chest angled forward like an arrow, his lungs filled with stormlust. His elbows were sharp at his side but not stiff.

Shut up legs, he commanded, Shut up and go go go!

He ran half blind through that sleazy downpour. His skin was cold to the touch, but he was the opposite of cold and the opposite of numb. He was a hot piece of ember. He sizzled. The cold, the rain, the field of dropped flies, the ruckus noise of coaches and trainers and runners calling for sideline support, that ominous feeling he had at the start - all of it turned him on. He channeled it, like he preached.

He charged the course.

For three hair-raising miles he went toe to toe with himself. He sucked whatever he could out of the thick air. His limbs were loose and his stride giant. While every head turned and waved for sideline support; while confusion reigned and coaches called paramedics and team trainers slid on their bottoms down the wet hills with first aid kits…the race went on, the clock kept running, and Kirby took the lead.

He led the field by far. In his childhood room he had posters on the walls of Wayne Gretzky, Michael Jordan, Steve Prefontaine. As he ran he could see those posters, see that room. On that homestretch, he was all three. He was Gretzky on the ice, Jordan midair, Prefontaine on the suicide pace…He was an ocean wave curling, a hornet's nest, a kid with drums on Christmas morning.

When he saw the final hill, he knew he was in striking distance. He was unstoppable. The course seemed to come at him as much as he went at it. How fast he was going, he did not know. Who was behind him, he did not know. Where his teammates were and how they were doing, he did not know.

What he did know was that he ran for them as much as for himself. What he did know is that his body and his desire were one. What he knew beyond doubt was that these were the grapes and this was the Kirby Spence he had been hiding in his back pocket for so long.

His face was relaxed and his eyes were soft. Holding his form, he hoofed it. As he hoofed it he carried a tune in his head. Frank Sinatra, The Summer Wind, a song his dad played in the backyard during the summers growing up, when he and his brothers would race from one end to the other, and he never won, His mom said, one day you will.

It was a song that boomed and ached, as he boomed and ached. The song was before him and behind him. It was above him and below him. It was under his skin and in his motion and in his mouth like the wine of desire.

Here it was: not the ten-string harp, but the church organ, notes thick as oak. Here it was: the heavy hand, the labor, the demon breath of stride he had all his life resisted. Here it was: pedal, forte, music to undress his soul.

He could see in his periphery other coaches diving off the sideline to check on their runners. He could see concerned parents and fans looking on. But he could also see his own Coach Cal, jumping outside their tent. His arms wheeled round and around. He leapt like a frog, shouted high above him words that drove him faster…Kirby Spence! Wheels wheels wheels! Kirby Spence! Wheels wheels wheels!

Again and again, Kirby leaned forward, addressing the rainslashed earth. As he approached the final hill he raised his level once more, dumped fuel on the fire. Years of embarrassment for his size, years of hanging his head in defeat, years of trying to train and contain his ungainly gallop into a tight, square, perfect running form - all of it fell to the wayside. He ran loose and haphazard. He smacked his lips and threw himself to the wind; gave himself over to that earlier, feral discipline called instinct. He abandoned pretty technique and ran ugly.

The rain, the wind, the unreadable course, all the clamor of elements could not touch him, could not slow him. The final hill neared the edge of the storm, and he ran rebelliously at it like he had the whole race, blind to its danger, deaf to its threat.

Not an ounce of him dragged. He was vagrant and beautiful through every limb. His motion harmonious. His running was a brute ballet.

He shrugged the cold, breasted ahead, fought his way upward. He took the hill, the nasty incline gorged with pockets of sludge. A sudden mudslide might bring him down, but he ran without fear and inhibition. He was clearheaded. For he ran with courage, and courage was a kind of hyperclarity - quieting the mind, calming his breath, giving his hammering feet purchase on the slick ground. The oncoming rain drove in his face, and he plunged ahead, alive and reckless, driven by the stormclouds overhead and stormclouds within.

He dug and dug, ran like a nightmare, and with all his power he came to the end.

The time keeper at the end was an old woman in a reflective vest and visor. She had been watching, like many, the commotion on the course and was surprised when he arrived and she checked the time.

She double-taked. Stared the big shivering giant up and down.

Mercy Minerva! she exclaimed, You made it through the

minefield. And a course record at that! That's All American speed right there.

Kirby smiled and wobbled in, in a daze of his own performance. The crowd was thin. Cal congratulated him heartily, gave him a handshake and words of affirmation. Kirby responded in kind, thanked him, made his way to the tent and toweled off. But he was still in that dreamy, racelike state. All the blood that had been pumping into his legs and arms, returned to the rest of his body. He tingled all over. He began to shiver and shake with runoff adrenaline.

He wrapped his towel around his shoulders and went out to watch the other runners come in. The next guy was far behind him.

The air at the finish was different than it was on the course. It was warmer. It looked like light at the bottom of the sea. The rain was different too. It was fine and misty. It had an older sound than it did on the course; a sweeter sound. It no longer battered. It came in gusts, sweeping through the vacated tents and bags, as though it surrendered, as though it accomplished its purpose. It swept through him too.

Without warning he took a knee. He was weary, wet, spent with joy. He chuckled from sheer exhaustion, then his eyes got hot, and he dropped his neck and sobbed into his elbow. When he got up, Momo came up behind him and pinched his skinny flank...

Kirby raised his eyes and Momo returned a funny look.

Were you having a moment? he said.

I guess I was...

I don't blame you. That was the craziest race I've ever seen. I walked the last mile through a field of strewn bodies. Some of them were saying some nasty stuff too. They looked bad.

What the hell was that?! Kirby said.

I'll tell you what, it wasn't rigor mortis. We can talk about *them* later, but for now let's talk about *you*.

He pushed him. You dog. You were the opposite of rigor mortis, Kirby. You were rigor Magis…you hear what I'm saying. Mortis couldn't touch you with a pole. That was *Magis*, baby, *Magis* all day long.

And he was right.

Sadness

A month passed. A lot can happen in a month. You could start at the end and reverse the days, retrace everything that happened up to the moment the last shreds of Paul's morals tore loose.

Shortly after the end of the race, the team found the empty bag of crushed pills on the soggy ground under the water cooler. Paul had dumped in a month's supply of his special sauce and mixed it with a paint stick. Everyone that took a sip before the race got a triple dose - not quite deadly, but close.

Kirby and Momo were the only ones who didn't drink the Kool-aid that day. It was ironic, even iconic, that the last guys up the hill at the start of the season were the first guys up at the end. Within hours of the end of the race, thankfully, mostly everyone recovered. The stags were dazed and confused. Their bodies were cramped and knotted. Dave described his leg as having three charlie horses in it.

But they were ok. They had vague memories of what happened and where they were. With a bit of iv hydration and rest, they were back on their feet. It remained a mystery what happened to the other runners on other teams who went down beside them that day. Some speculated it was a true instance of mass hysteria; when some guys saw other guys going down, the power of suggestion hit them too like a 2 by 4.

Still, the Stags had no recollection. Whole hours before the race went missing from their memory. Tyson told Kirby he couldn't remember lifting his hand at the starting line. And the more they learned about what happened the more their missing memories seemed like a strange mercy.

Paul was the only one in critical condition. Halfway through the rigged race he fled the scene and crashed his dad's car doing 60 miles an hour on a slick back road.

His world went blank. He went into a coma for 48 hours.

During the first day of those 48 hours, the team visited him in the afternoon. They sat around in chairs and listened to the medical equipment beep. They brought no flowers, no food. No one took his hand or cried like they do in the movies. They just sat forward in their chairs, each of them looking soberly at his closed eyes, hoping to see a flicker.

The whole season arrived at that moment. Time stood still. All the preceding drama, contention, stripped records and old coaches, was consumed in that deathly quiet, in those shut eyes. The season and all its results became as insignificant and small as the head of a pin.

After a long thirty minutes, Momo whispered those fateful words to Tits, who was sitting next to him.

What if he doesn't wake up?

Tits gave him a sharp nudge and said, curtly, Don't talk - as if he were ashamed to hear the question. A few minutes later, they all got up and filed out. They heard beeps and more beeps down the hall. They left that day and waited and waited.

During that time they thought about the year. They thought about all the strategies they had used to bring Paul down. Now they didn't want to bring him down. They wanted to bring him back. They wondered if they saw him, if he would revert to the way he had been all year. If he would be driven by the same resentment, or worse. They prayed and hoped and waited. They walked on eggshells, the whole team.

They also learned more about the drug they were slipped. It wasn't good news. It was originally manufactured as a study drug, a more powerful alternative to Adderall. Though it was never designed to be used with intense physical exertion, at some point it was co-opted by a few high school football players in Tampa and made its way up the Eastern seaboard. Early adopters found the results of the drug exceptional and the symptoms mild. But by the time the Glit reached Loyola high, most of the pills were knockoffs laced with filler drugs - sometimes fatal filler drugs.

All the symptoms added up: quiets the bionoise, wipes memory, seizes muscles, inhibits the frontal lobes (which explained why so many of them had filthy mouths for days after, before it passed out of their system.)

None of this was reassuring. None of it strengthened their hope in Paul's recovery.

Gimp

Finally they got the news. He was back. He was alive and well. Not perfectly well. But well enough to leave in a few days. He was being mended, sewed up, put together again.

Soon they would see him.

The middle of the month rolled around, and they saw him two days after he checked out of the hospital. They met him at his house. He came out like a walking mummy. He wore a neck brace, tape around his head. He had dentures, screws in his shoulder, a shattered arm in full cast, a foot boot…a fractured rib.

They couldn't believe it was him. He hobbled over to where they stood, the rest of them. One of his eyes was black and blue and almost shut. His voice, when he spoke, sounded different because of his new false teeth.

How are you, Sam said. Can't believe it's you.

He raised his big green arm cast, put it down.

Can't believe it's me either. How do I look?

Like a gimp, Momo said.

A lucky gimp, Felix said.

Paul laughed, but it hurt to laugh with his fractured ribs. He sucked a little air through his mouth. When he looked up at Felix he got choked up. Tears came to his eyes, even his black one. He tried to lower his head, realized he couldn't with his neck brace, so he choked up in front of all of them. Tears rolled down his face, from nowhere. He couldn't wipe his eyes easily with either hand or elbow, so he turned his back, and said, Sorry, and the tears came again, a fresh flood.

He stood with his back to them, his shoulders shaking a little. Tits came around and handed him a napkin. Paul was impeded with all his bandages, so Tits took the liberty to mop his eyes for gingerly him, and his nose.

Momo said, Tits, why do you always have napkins in your pocket?

Paul laughed again, and winced because it hurt to laugh. When he had calmed some, he turned around and told them the medical staff said it was a miracle he was there, considering the evidence of the crash. His dad's car was crumpled like a soda can. The steering wheel split in two, and the wreckage units said they had never seen a wheel split like that.

What else did they tell you?

They said if I hadn't been so relaxed at the point of impact I could have died.

No one needed to ask why he was so relaxed.

Miracle, he kept saying. Miracle...

Not only that, Dave said. Look there, you still got your legs. Completely untouched. Plenty of miles left on those puppies, huh.

Paul blew a heavy breath out. He said, I'll be glad to take a break from all that for a while...

Then he hobbled up to them one by one and extended the tips of his fingers, which was all that he could manage through his cast. He shook their hands and said, I'm sorry, I'm sorry,

I'm sorry, to each one of them, all the way down the line, until he reached Momo. When he reached Momo he lifted his lips revealing his new teeth.

Momo said, They're very nice. You're not going to blame me for your dentures, are you?

Paul said, My memory is shot and screwed up. Especially the last few weeks. But when they were putting these on I kept thinking of you for some reason. I don't know why. Whatever I did, whatever I said. I'm sorry.

He looked around at the rest of them. You all can whip my ass when I'm recovered…

Oh no, esse. Momo said, We'll be doing it before that, just wait…

Before…what's that mean? he said.

Just wait…

Coach Cal

It's true. It was a miracle that Paul was walking, talking, wincing, flashing his new teeth. As he convalesced, there was even a running joke that on that race day the stags had turned to fainting goats. But the real miracle, his team observed, was the change of heart, the unaccountable shift in his attitude. He emerged from the hospital a different person than when he entered.

He was cut with remorse. Real remorse. He was a dog that had lost its bark. Although his memory was only a broken recollection of days and weeks, of events and sensations - he seemed to feel a tremendous guilt toward it. He had an intuition of what had happened, of what he'd done. He was haunted, humbled by an overwhelming sense of contrition.

They could see it in his eyes, in his face, in the way he moved, in the tears he cried with his back turned. They had never seen Paul cry. They had seen him bitter, angry, mad. They had seen him confident, cocky, possessed of ambition. They had seen how every perceived threat and escalating challenge roused his intensity another notch.

They had never seen him sad. When sadness overtook him, his face, so furrowed with discipline and seriousness, turned soft and puffy, like a boxer after a fight.

In his sadness he came to see Coach Cal one afternoon. What he intended to say, he did not know and he did not plan. But he needed to say something. He needed to get something off his chest.

When he came to the office the door was cracked. A light was on. Paul knocked with the wrist of his cast and Cal opened it and welcomed him in. Paul felt a cold, brief draft of fear, coming into that office, which was Presses - but it passed when he walked through the door. The room was different. The walls were plain and undecorated. The shelves were clear. There was a clean desk and a neat stack of papers and two chairs. Cal pulled a chair up for Paul.

May I sit, Paul said.

You may sit…

Paul sat down, adjusted his sling.

What brings you in Paul?

Paul stared at the ground and his leg began to bounce restless. All that he felt, all the undisclosed emotion swirling in his thoughts came rushing to his head and into his bruised broken body. He swallowed hard, tried to put one word in front of the next before saying anything, but what came out instead was his cast arm making a swift blow on his leg.

The words jumped out, If I wouldn't have sabotaged…If I wouldn't have…

The leg continued to bounce, the eyes continued to stare, the mouth continued to move like it was knotted with words…

Paul, Cal said calmly, Are you here to come to terms with what you've done?

Again the cast came down harder on his leg…answering for him…

Paul, that's enough. Slow down and look at me. Here, he

said. He scooted forward and repositioned Paul's cast on the arm rest, so he wouldn't swing it again.

All I've done is saba...

Stop! Cal raised his voice. Stop saying that. Please. Drop that word from your vocabulary. It won't do you any good to keep repeating it. Now I'm not here to condone or excuse anything you did. You hurt a lot of people, but most of all you hurt yourself. And you'll hurt yourself more if you keep telling yourself you're a saboteur. It's not the way I see it and it's not the way your team sees it.

The way I see it is you got sick with envy. Then you turned and took it out on others. And you made them sick because of it. Quite literally. But your team wasn't cussing you behind your back. They weren't. They were scared for you. They were just hoping you woke up.

Envy? Paul scowled. I wasn't envious...

Weren't you? Didn't all this begin the day the new guy arrived.

It wasn't him, it was Press.

Sure, Press may have triggered it, but would you really have gone to the length you did, if Felix was just some bum runner and you remained on top of the heap the whole year?

Paul was quiet.

Right...I doubt it. You might have thought you were taking it out on him, but it dragged everybody down. Felix took nothing from you Paul. Nothing. Why can't you see that? You took it from yourself. All year long you went around like he was your enemy, your rival, the guy out to get you - and he wasn't any of that. He was your teammate, and just a ridiculously fast runner. It's as simple as that.

Paul sat back in his chair with his cast and arm sling resting on his stomach. He had a hard time looking at Cal, but it was clear he understood and agreed with what was being said.

Most people will never have your trouble, Paul. Most of the guys who come out for the team and run cross country. The Momo's and Tit's of the world. That's no knock on them. But when you're as fast as you are, and as disciplined too, it's easy to take for granted. It's easy to put all your eggs into the basket, thinking your talent's your gift to the world. It can consume your whole life.

Yeah, too bad I choked it all away, Paul said in a heartless way. There's nothing worse than choking…

Sure there is. Quitting is. Giving up is. Cursing everything you've worked for. To choke at all you've got to be there. There's plenty of good runners who never get a chance to choke because they're always hanging in the middle or back of the pack. You don't choke when you're sitting back there. You choke when you've got something at stake.

You ever heard of the Yerkes Dodson graph?

Paul shook his head.

He opened the drawer and pulled out a sheet with a bell curve on it.

Sounds academic, but it's not complicated. Look here. The X axis was labeled arousal (anxiety). The Y axis was labeled Performance.

Cal said, Historically psychologists thought people performed their best when their skills and ability met a certain amount of pressure. Arousal, anxiety, nerves… same thing.

And they thought performance diminished at a certain point, he traced the top of the curve as it began to did, when the pressure got too big

What I want you to think is this...

He took a pen and drew a line over the graph that followed the first half of the bell, but continued sloping upward when the other dipped. Then he drew a dotted line between the line that rose and the bell that fell back.

The space between these two lines is what the old boys call attitude. It's how you approach your challenge. It's your interpretation of pressure. If I were you I'd lean in to your challenge. Start going towards it. It's not just in running. It's in everything. The more you go towards it, the easier it gets. The more you go away, the harder. You can turn it all around, Paul. if you choose. That's the simple thing, and the hard thing. It's your *choice*.

The drug you took and you gave to your teammates does this, and he drew a sharp horizontal line across the graph. It flatlines the curve. It makes an artificial ceiling, so that you can't feel the nerves, and the gut wrenching anticipation of being on the line. Or mid race, when your lungs are maxed out and you feel someone at your heels gaining. And you feel like you can't give any more.

I get why guys take it. But here's the thing: the moment you separate the horror from the glory, you emasculate both. When you take that away, you strangle the beauty of running, the battle of it. Running is a battle, a beautiful battle. And when you strip away the dread feeling you bastardize the most beautiful thing about it if you're not careful. That, to me, is the very best part of this sport.

You may have PR'd. You may have set another record. So what? If you never felt yourself beating yourself, subduing your passion and passing your old barrier of limitation, does it really matter what your time is. You knew it'd be a lie. Even if you won't admit to yourself.

He took his hat off and shaped his hand into it like a baseball glove.

I would never want that for you, Paul.

Cal looked at him, unsure what he was thinking. Paul's head hadn't turned for minutes. His eyes stared. His lips were shut. He looked dejected, like he had learned the hard lesson but was unsure what to do with it. Like he passed the threshold of his despair, but was lost.

Cal put his hat on and stuck his hand out. He wanted to embrace Paul, to show him some tenderness. Paul looked down at the hand then, then reached slowly with the fingers at the end of his cast and shook it. Paul gripped tight for a moment, then his strength gave and the tears began rolling down his face, the way they had with the team. He couldn't stop them.

There you go, that's alright big guy. Don't worry about that. Cal leaned forward and Paul fell into him, cast and sling and brace and all, like a boy defeated after a ball game. He leaned his head against Cal's shoulder and sobbed until his nose was snotty and soaked through with tears.

Cal pat him on the back over and over. Then he helped prop him up. He looked the kid clear in the face. Paul rubbed his eyes with the end of his shirt.

What do I do, Coach? After all this? he mumbled.

It was the first time Paul called him coach.

Coach Cal smiled. He said, It might sound like contradictory advice, but I'd say keep running. Go from here and live your life to the full. Start today. Pretend all your records here were just practice…

Practice for what?

For the rest of your races. On the track and off…

Paul sniffled, considering that.

Coach Cal looked tenderly toward him, knowing it was tenderness Paul needed more than anything else.

So leave it all behind? Paul said. Is that what you mean?

No, Cal said. Paul turned to him, surprised.

Take it all with you. All the good that Press taught. Bring it with you, he said. Don't throw it away. There are many things Press could teach you that I could not teach you, even if I had you for four more years.

One thing I hope you do take from me is to work hard, but save some patience for yourself, especially when you're down in the mouth. If you can, try to forgive Press. He was a great coach who made a great mistake. Then go forth and stand up on your two legs first of all. It's alright to get down sometimes, but don't stay down. Show the world you're not a comeback story, you're not a headline, a hasbeen, or some chariots of fire burnout going nowhere fast. Get back to running and taking your sport seriously. And that means accepting you won't do it all perfectly. It will take time. Take your time…Whatever you do, don't look for the shortcut. Sometimes there's no shortcut out of hell. Sometimes the shortcut is the hell.

He took his hat off, worked his hand into it, thinking of anything else he wanted to add. He said, It may not seem this way now, but this year might be the best year that ever happened to you, Paul. If you'll learn from it. I'll tell you something…something I've learned from a few extra years under my belt. You never really leave high school. Sure, you go on and do other things and meet new people, but the same desires are there no matter what. The wanting to be part of the in crowd, the jealousies, the disappointments, the ambition…

the girl who gives you the runaround.

Paul laughed at the way Cal said, The girl who gives you the runaround, and the laughter made his ribs throb. But it was a sweet throb, and it was what he needed. He needed some laughter.

Paul stood up and they shook hands again, exchanged a look of camaraderie. For the first time all season Paul felt like he could finally appreciate Coach Cal for who he was. Not a bruiser. Not a fanatic. Not a legend, myth, or some god among coaches.

He was a coach. Just a coach. A coach with a heart.

And that made all the difference.

Hoyas

At the end of his frail rope Coach Cal gave him a knot to hold onto. And Felix gave him another. It was something he didn't expect. Something he had not counted on. A long shot. A twist in his luck.

Felix sent him a curious text one afternoon.

The text read, How do you like the Hoyas?

For what? he wrote back.

For you.

??

We should talk…

That night Felix called him.

He said, Paul, I might have done something.

Done something? Is that good or bad?

That's up to you, I think.

Paul could hear some excitement on the other end of the line. Paul was sitting on the floor against the side of his bed, watching television. He turned it off.

Go on, he said.

Felix explained that he had pitched Paul to the track coach at Georgetown.

Pitched me for what?

To run - cross country!

He faltered, I can't…I'm not…
Paul!
What?
He knows. He knows all the stuff. All of it. I explained it. He wants to talk to you in person, but the deal is, if you're interested, you might have a spot. There'd be a year of probation. Basically, you could practice but not compete for that first year. But after that…green lights.
Green lights?
Green lights…we'd be teammates too…if you decide to.

There was a muffled sound on the other end. Felix couldn't hear him anymore.
Paul, are you still there?

In his disbelief, Paul went silent. Then he tucked his sling arm close to his ribs and started laughing, laughing and hurting and laughing to the point he was almost crying…
Paul, you there? What do you think…
I'm here, I'm here…I got no words right now, but I'm green lights all the way…

New start

Beneath his bangs and bruises, beneath the rigid braces and stiff slings, Paul was like a tender green sprout poking through the hard earth. Life was returning to him slowly. And not just life in neutral, but life in a higher gear.

He was going to be a Hoya. He was going to run four more years beside Felix Sun, who he could not possibly hate anymore.

He was going to use his probationary year to start again, to take it all as practice, as Coach Cal put it. All of it excited him, all of it felt ripe with opportunity, with new beginning. Paul Stafford was a dead man come to life. He was ready to throw off all his bandages and start.

But first, there was something they needed to do.

In lieu of an end of year banquet, the boys decided to host another team trip. Retreat 2.0, they called it…

Paul had no say in the planning of it, and after the way the first one went, he preferred it that way. In fact they told him nothing except pack your bags and be ready to go. So he did. Friday evening, Tits and Momo showed up in his driveway and he limped out. Momo got out and took his bag for him and threw it in the trunk, and opened the door and helped Paul in the backseat.

He joked, Paul, now that you're gimped up and immobile, I feel like I'm especially your little Latino bellhop.

Are you going to tell me where we're going? They said, nope. They said, take a nap and we'll be there eventually.

There was no pee bush this time. It was a pee dune this time. Instead of the cold, rocky coast of Maine, they rented a beach house in Corolla, North Carolina, on the Outer Banks. A big brown house on stilts. It was far away from the nearest tourist traps, and right on the water. They had the beach to themselves.

During the daytime they swam and skimboarded and ate donuts on the beach. They dug manholes and played bocce and talked about girls. Mostly on that front they peppered Kirby with questions about Kara and he peppered them back with lines from poems he had been reading.

Since when do you read poems, Dave dug at him.

Since he's in love, Sam answered for him…

The big guy didn't deny it. He put on his wide brimmed hat and layered on thick goops of sunscreen for his fair skin.

In the afternoon there were drinking games and board games and beer pong. There was Frank Sinatra on the boombox and country hits on the boombox and there was Taylor Swift karaoke before dinner. Grilled meats and golden fries and baked beans.

After dinner, Kirby let air out of the tires and drove the dragon on to the beach. Ultimate frisbee in the gold failing dusk. They played in the headlights drawing big loping shadows and silhouettes across the thick sand. The teams were shirts and skins, but really, they were all skins.

The next day they hit repeat.

They got sunburns and dragged sand into the house and undercooked their hotdogs in boiling water. They walked shirtless and danced shirtless and sunbathed without sunscreen. They buried each other in sand, and wrestled on the surf and talked about girls. They bodysurfed the cold salty water and came out drenched in sun and smiles. And they ran. They marked off hundred meter dashes with driftwood and took turns busting balls. They ran. They ran in lala land.

The second night, Felix performed his dance routine on the beach before the fire pit. When he was done the floor opened and Sam said, Alright, who's next?

Tits got up and Tyson, who was playing DJ, stopped the music.

I got something for you, Tits.

I'm not doing it alone, he said.

Fine, then grab a partner.

Dave and Sam snuck behind Paul and hoisted him up.

Oh, hell no!

Oh, hell yes!

Tits was waiting for him, by the fire. He had on red lifeguard trunks and his hair stood up like a troll doll and his smiling cheeks were red as apples and his man Tits were soft and bouncy.

His arms were open in the position of a waltz, and it was towards this firelit, waltz-figure Tits that Sam and Dave pushed their old captain.

Paul couldn't believe he was doing this, that he was stooping to this, but he knew it was exactly what they wanted and what he deserved, and so he gave in. He swallowed his pride and assumed the position with his cast hand clasped in Tit's. He cracked a real smile and it was the first time they saw him smile like that all year. When he complained that his foot might not move well in the sand, that his ribs would hurt, Tits said, Hush honey, we'll go nice and slow.

This was Paul's penance. He knew it, and he took and he honored it.

Tyson started the music. A big walloping twang right from the start. Not a waltz, a square dance. Tits led and Paul followed. They walked to the square dance; they square danced to the waltz. Around the team and around the ring of fire they went.

I can't take it anymore! Paul said. Can someone rescue me?! His Tits are bouncing, his hand is sweaty, he's smiling at me like a gayboy and his breath smells like ketchup!

There were whistles and claps. Paul shook free and took his seat, and continued shaking his head, shaking the ketchup breath off him

Paul Stafford, ladies and gentleman, Momo called out, Paul Stafford…

That night they stayed up listening to music and talking till the fire went out. Dave took a cooled ember and was the first to chalk his name on Paul's arm cast. He passed it around, and others signed it too: *'magis'*, they wrote, *'blame it on the jacket'*, *'antonio'*, 'rayman, a few crude (later smudged out) pictures courtesy of Tits.

Kirby wrote something on the elbow that was hard to read.

NEW START

Paul turned his arm to the fire.
What's it say?
Sing up, heart…
Sing up, heart?
Yep.
What's that from?
A poem I read recently.
You mean one of your love poems for Kara Klein?
Nope, he chuckled. That one's for you, Paul.

Primal Scream

By the end of their long weekend, they were hungry and they did not feel it. They were thirsty, uncomfortable, cold, sleep deprived. They used toilet rolls for pillows and hand towels for covers, and none of this they noticed or felt as an impoverishment. They were rich, they were together, there was laughter in every conversation and heaps of pure, good natured nonsense and drunken bets.

It was health to their souls. They could look back on a grueling year, a dramatic year, and count it the finest time yet, a high point from which all their toils and heartbreaks seemed like trifles, and all their losses seemed like wins, and all the dust they ate like red meat, and all the pain a passing thing, a shadow of that more beautiful excellence: of being free and fast and young, of being men and friends together.

Once more they had fallen under that spell other runners talked about, that ache to go back to the start of the year, back to the beginning, to the dog days of summer, to the whistle, to the murderous hills and intervals, to speed workouts and broken wills and glorious slogs.

There was still one thing more to do.

At three am the morning of the last day, they appeared at

Paul's bedside, all of them, like a team of bandits. Momo took the edge of Paul's bedsheet and brought it to his nose to tickle. When he awoke to all their heads surrounding him, he jerked, twanged his ribs and bit down on his lip.

Hell are you doing right now?!

Kirby pushed forward and said, Don't fight it Paul…don't fight it. You're coming with us.

He picked him up on the spot and the others assisted, some taking his legs and others his arms. Momo followed behind with a pair of green garden shears he found in the outdoor closet. Paul caught a glimpse of it as they carried him down the back steps to the beach.

What's that for, he said. What's he got those for?

You'll see.

All day the sky had been a flawless blue and that night it remained a flawless blue, only darker. The ocean was calm and the moon was bright. They set him down in the sand and Momo made a couple terrifying practice clips in the air. He came forward with a dirty look on his face, like a Latino henchman. Paul was cornered.

Momo pretended like he was opening the shears around Paul's manparts, then he smiled and said, Just kidding, we're not that insane. Tits, Kirby, and Felix came behind Paul and extended his cast out to the side. Held it in place.

Momo said, on behalf of this team, we're saying goodbye to this sucker and all its cat litter stench.

Paul, though he was still shocked, did not object.

Watch it! he yelled, don't snip my fingers.

Then shut up and let me cut.

It was not a sharp pair of shears. They bent, twisted, chewed, and gnawed their way through the green cast. But at last they got through. When it was severed through, they pried it off and kicked sand on it.

How do you feel? Sam said.

Paul looked at his pale arm, Naked, he said.

Good.

Upon that word, all of them dropped their drawers to their ankles and swung their shirts off and huddled in the buff.

We got one last primal scream in us this year, Paul. You obviously can't run it with us, but we have an important task for you.

Yes?

They pointed at Felix…

This kid needs a name.

A name?

A *name...*

They need not say another word. He knew what they meant. Without further ado, the bundles of farmer's tans and white cheeks jiggled down where the sand was packed. They looked back at Paul and gave him a thumbs up. Then they went.

A naked haze. Footprints. Cold flaps of flesh. Goosebumps. Shouts. Squeals. Ocean spray and chilly mist. Whistles and windbeat. The soft drum of feet on the earth. Dancing noodles.

Watching them tear off, Paul had never felt such a lust for running. He could feel his spared legs twitching with the ghost of motion. He watched them go. Watched the trail of sand dancing behind them. Watched as they melted away into moonlight and darkness.

The spirit of their streak was like the spirit of a kid riding his bike down a hill. After a few pedals, the hill takes over and all he does is put his arms out like wings. It was like that.

With his skinny pale arm that smelled like cat litter, hanging at his side, Paul tugged his rotten cast down the surf and kicked it in. He watched it drift off slowly into the calm sea like a dead limb. As he watched it drift away, he thought of all the names written on it, now washed away. He thought if he could write one more name on it, one more name for the kid who wrecked his life and saved it, what would it be?

Then it came to him and he had it. He had the name.

The pack was coming back. He could see the figures getting bigger, faster. What began in silliness got serious. The strides tightened, the superfluous motion pared away. They were booking it home. The wind was against them and their hairdos flared back like they were being hit by a gigantic blow dryer.

Paul started after them. He started shouting, SQUIRRELMEAT! SQUIRRELMEAT! SQUIRRELMEAT! at the top of his lungs. As he closed the gap he kept shouting it, kept holding his ribs. Whether they heard him or not did not matter, because that was the name, and it was perfect, because the uglier the name the better the runner.

He shouted until his voice grew hoarse. Then he stopped and watched them run. They ran not as many, but as one. And he knew something. He knew all living things, all flying birds and fish that swam in the deep, and things that crept in the earth, and those that lived under the earth should be like those runners with bodies reconciled to gravity. He knew that every man who runs free from fear runs naked, runs at ease in the garden of Eden - becomes a pulse of pure light radiating from the center and throbbing like the strings of a sweet violin. That's what he knew.

A note from the author

Dear reader,

Thank you for reading. It's a joy to tell stories and share them with you. I look forward to sharing more soon. If you've enjoyed this book, I'd love to read your thoughts in a review. For updates about new releases and special giveaways, sign up for the newsletter on my website: mattballeza.com

Much appreciated!

Matthew's books on Amazon:
https://www.amazon.com/author/matthewballeza

About the Author

Matthew Balleza grew up along the waterways of Annapolis, MD. He now lives with his wife and children in Nashville, TN. He writes stories for adults and young readers alike. His go-to dad line is, 'I'm just a thorn among roses.' (which is true). In his free time he loves playing tennis, fishing, and concocting specialty cocktails.

You can connect with me on:
- https://mattballeza.com
- https://www.instagram.com/mattballezabooks

Printed in Great Britain
by Amazon